Working Papers

for

Financial Accounting

Second Edition

J. David Spiceland
University of Memphis

Wayne Thomas
University of Oklahoma

Don Herrmann
Oklahoma State University

Working Papers for
FINANCIAL ACCOUNTING
J. David Spiceland, Wayne Thomas, and Don Herrmann

Published by McGraw-Hill/Irwin, an imprint of The McGraw-Hill Companies, Inc., 1221 Avenue of the Americas, New York, NY 10020. Copyright © 2011, 2009 by The McGraw-Hill Companies, Inc. All rights reserved.

1 2 3 4 5 6 7 8 9 0 QDB/QDB 1 0 9 8 7 6 5 4 3 2 1 0

ISBN: 978-0-07-732825-2
MHID: 0-07-732825-6

www.mhhe.com

Contents

Contents

Exercise 1-1

Transactions	Business Activity
1. Borrow from the bank.	_____
2. Provide services to customers.	_____
3. Issue common stock to investors.	_____
4. Purchase land.	_____
5. Pay rent for the current period.	_____
6. Pay dividends to stockholders.	_____
7. Purchase building.	_____

Exercise 1-2

Transaction	Account	Activity
1. Falcon purchases common stock of Wildcat.	_____	_____
2. Falcon borrows from Wildcat by signing a note.	_____	_____
3. Wildcat pays dividends to Falcon.	_____	_____
4. Falcon provides services to Wildcat.	_____	_____
5. Falcon pays interest to Wildcat on borrowing.	_____	_____

Exercise 1-3

Transaction	Account	Activity
1. Falcon purchases common stock of Wildcat.	_____	_____
2. Falcon borrows from Wildcat by signing a note.	_____	_____
3. Wildcat pays dividends to Falcon.	_____	_____
4. Falcon provides services to Wildcat.	_____	_____
5. Falcon pays interest to Wildcat on borrowing.	_____	_____

Name _____ Date _____ Course _____ Section _____

Exercise 1-4

Requirement 1:

	–		=	Net Income

Requirement 2:

	=		+	Stockholders' equity

Exercise 1-5

Requirement 1:

	–		=	Net Loss

Requirement 2:

	=		+	Stockholders' equity

Exercise 1-6

Cow Boy Law Firm Income Statement		
Net income		

Name _____ Date _____ Course _____ Section _____

Exercise 1-7

Buffalo Drilling Statement of Stockholders' Equity			
	Common Stock	Retained Earnings	Total Stockholders' Equity
Beginning Balance			
Ending Balance			

Exercise 1-8

Wolfpack Construction Balance Sheet			
Assets		**Liabilities**	
Total assets		Total liabilities and stockholders' equity	

Exercise 1-9

Requirement 1

Beginning balance	
Ending balance	

Name _____ Date _____ Course _____ Section _____

Exercise 1-9 Continued

Requirement 2

Tiger Trade Statement of Cash Flows		
Cash Flows from Operating Activities		
Cash Flows from Investing Activities		
Cash Flows from Financing Activities		
Net increase in cash		
Cash at the beginning of the year		
Cash at the end of the year		

Exercise 1-10

1.		−		=	Net Income

2.		=		+	Net income	−	Dividends

3.		=		+	Stockholders' equity

4.	Total change in cash		=		+		+	Financing cash flows

 Financial Accounting

Name _____ Date _____ Course _____ Section _____

Exercise 1-11

Year	Net Income	Dividends	Retained Earnings
1.			
2.			
3.			
4.			
5.			

Exercise 1-12

Coca-Cola

1.		=		−	Dividends

Pepsico

2.		=		−	Net Income

Google

3.		=		−	Dividends

Sirius Satellite Radio

4.	Ending retained earnings	=		−	

Abercrombie & Fitch

5.	Beginning in retained earnings	=		−	

Exercise 1-13

ExxonMobil

1.	Assets		Liabilities		Stockholders' equity

Citigroup

2.	Assets		Liabilities		Stockholders' equity

Amazon.com

3.	Assets		Liabilities		Stockholders' equity

Nike

4.	Change in Assets		Change in Liabilities		Change in stockholders' equity

Kellogg

5.	Change in Assets		Change in Liabilities		Change in stockholders' equity

Name _____ Date _____ Course _____ Section _____

Exercise 1-14

Kraft Foods

1.	Total change in cash		Operating cash flows		Investing cash flows		Financing cash flows

Sara Lee

2.	Total change in cash		Operating cash flows		Investing cash flows		Financing cash flows

Performance Food Group

3.	Total change in cash		Operating cash flows		Investing cash flows		Financing cash flows

Smithfield Foods

4.	Total change in cash		Operating cash flows		Investing cash flows		Financing cash flows

Tyson Foods

5.	Total change in cash		Operating cash flows		Investing cash flows		Financing cash flows

The McGraw-Hill Companies *Financial Accounting*

Name _____ Date _____ Course _____ Section _____

Exercise 1-15

Independent Situations	Qualitative Characteristics

1. In deciding whether to invest in Southwest Airlines or American Airlines, investors evaluate the companies' income statements.

   _____

2. To provide the most reliable information about future sales, Walmart 's management provides unbiased estimates of the decline in inventory value each year.

   _____

3. In deciding whether to loan money, Wells Fargo uses balance sheet information to forecast the probability of bankruptcy.

   _____

4. IBM is required to issue public financial statements within 60 days of its year end.

   _____

5. Employees of Starbucks can use the company's financial statements to understand the efficiency with which management has conducted operations over the past year.

   _____

6. When first requiring firms to prepare a statement of cash flows, the FASB's intent was not to discourage or promote investment in the automobile industry.

   _____

7. When Harley-Davidson reports revenue for the year, the amount includes sales not only in the United States but also those outside the United States.

   _____

8. The amount of total assets reported by General Mills can be substantiated by its auditors.

   _____

9. The Cheesecake Factory prepares its balance sheet in a clear format using basic accounting terminology to allow users to easily comprehend the company's assets, liabilities, and stockholders' equity.

   _____

Exercise 1-16

1. _____ Economic entity   a. A common denominator is needed to measure all business activities.

2. _____ Going concern   b. Economic events can be identified with a particular economic body.

3. _____ Periodicity   c. In the absence of information to the contrary, it is anticipated that a business entity will continue to operate indefinitely.

4. _____ Monetary unit   d. The economic life of a company can be divided into artificial time intervals for financial reporting.

Name _____ Date _____ Course _____ Section _____

Problem 1-1A

Type of Business Activity	Transactions
1. _____	Pay amount owed to the bank for previous borrowing
2. _____	Pay utility costs
3. _____	Purchase equipment to be used in operations
4. _____	Provide services to customers
5. _____	Purchase office supplies
6. _____	Purchase a building
7. _____	Pay workers salaries
8. _____	Pay for research and development costs
9. _____	Pay taxes to the IRS
10. _____	Sell common stock to investors

Problem 1-2A

Account Classifications	Related Transactions	Account Names
1. _____	Sale of common stock to investors	Common Stock
2. _____	Machines used for operations	Machines
3. _____	Amounts owed to employees	Salaries Payable
4. _____	Sales of services to customers	Service Revenue
5. _____	Cost of utilities	Utilities Expense
6. _____	Purchase of rent one year in advance	Prepaid Rent
7. _____	Cost of research and development	Research and development expense
8. _____	Property used for operations.	Land
9. _____	Amounts owed to the IRS for federal income taxes.	Federal income taxes payable
10. _____	Amount of interest owed on borrowing.	Interest Payable

Name _____ Date _____ Course _____ Section _____

Problem 1-3A

Longhorn Corporation		
Income Statement		
Net income		

Longhorn Corporation			
Statement of Stockholders' Equity			
	Common Stock	Retained Earnings	Total Stockholders' Equity
Balance at January 1			
Balance at January 31			

Longhorn Corporation			
Balance Sheet			
Assets		**Liabilities**	
Total assets		Total liabilities and stockholders' equity	

Problem 1-4A

BullDog, Inc. Income Statement	
Net income	

BullDog, Inc. Statement of Stockholders' Equity		
	Common Stock	Retained Earnings
Beginning bal.		
Ending bal.		

BullDog, Inc. Balance Sheet			
Assets		**Liabilities**	
		Stockholders' Equity	
Total assets		Total liabilities and stockholders' equity	

Name _____ Date _____ Course _____ Section _____

Problem 1-5A

Cornhusker Company Income Statement For the year ended December 31, 2012		
Net income		

Cornhusker Company Statement of Stockholders' Equity For the year ended December 31, 2012			
	Common Stock	**Retained Earnings**	**Total Stockholders'**
Beginning Balance			
Ending Balance			

Cornhusker Company Balance Sheet December 31, 2012			
Assets		**Liabilities**	
		Stockholders' Equity	
Total assets		Total liabilities and stockholders' equity	

 Financial Accounting

Name _____ Date _____ Course _____ Section _____

Problem 1-6A

Assumption violated

1. _____

2. _____

3. _____

4. _____

Problem 1-7A

Terms	Definitions
1. _____ Completeness	a. Requires the consideration of the costs and value of information.
2. _____ Comparability	b. Ability to make comparisons between firms.
3. _____ Neutrality	c. Comprehending the meaning of accounting information.
4. _____ Consistency	d. Including all information necessary to report the business activity.
5. _____ Cost effectiveness	e. The business will last indefinitely unless there is evidence otherwise.
6. _____ Verifiability	f. Recording transactions only for the company.
7. _____ Decision usefulness	g. Implies consensus among different measures.
8. _____ Economic entity assumption	h. Accounting should be useful in making decisions.
9. _____ Going concern assumption	i. Accounting information should not favor a particular group.

 Financial Accounting

Name _____ Date _____ Course _____ Section _____

Problem 1-1B

Type of business activity	Transactions
1. _____	Pay for advertising
2. _____	Pay dividends to stockholders
3. _____	Collect cash from customer for previous sale
4. _____	Purchase a building to be used for operations.
5. _____	Purchase equipment.
6. _____	Sell land.
7. _____	Receive a loan from the bank by signing a note.
8. _____	Pay suppliers for purchase of supplies.
9. _____	Provide services to customers
10. _____	Invest in securities of another company.

Problem 1-2B

Account Classifications	Account Names	Related Transactions
1. _____	Cash	Receive cash from customers
2. _____	Service Revenue	Provide services to customers
3. _____	Prepaid Insurance	Purchase insurance in advance
4. _____	Buildings	Purchase factory for operations
5. _____	Advertising Expense	Pay for cost of advertising
6. _____	Equipment	Purchase equipment for operations
7. _____	Interest Expense	Pay for cost of interest
8. _____	Accounts Payable	Purchase supplies on credit
9. _____	Dividends	Distribute cash to stockholders
10. _____	Notes Payable	Borrow from the bank

The McGraw-Hill Companies *Financial Accounting*

Problem 1-3B

Gator Investments		
Income Statement		
Net income		

	Common Stock	Retained Earnings	Total Stockholders' Equity
Gator Investments			
Statement of Stockholders' Equity			
Beginning Balance			
Ending Balance			

Assets		Liabilities	
Gator Investments			
Balance Sheet			
		Stockholders' Equity	
Total assets		Total liabilities and stockholders' equity	

Name _____ Date _____ Course _____ Section _____

Problem 1-4B

CYCLONE, INC. Income Statement	
Net income	

CYCLONE, INC. Statement of Stockholders' Equity		
	Common Stock	**Retained Earnings**
Beginning bal.		
Ending bal.		

CYCLONE, INC. Balance Sheet			
Assets		**Liabilities**	
		Stockholders' Equity	
Total assets		Total liabilities and stockholders' equity	

Name _____ Date _____ Course _____ Section _____

Problem 1-5B

Tar Heel Corporation Income Statement For the year ended December 31, 2012		
Net income		

Tar Heel Corporation Statement of Stockholders' Equity For the year ended December 31, 2012			
	Common Stock	**Retained Earnings**	**Total Stockholders' Equity**
Beginning Balance			
Ending Balance			

Tar Heel Corporation Balance Sheet December 31, 2012			
Assets		**Liabilities**	
		Stockholders' Equity	
Total assets		Total liabilities and stockholders' equity	

The McGraw-Hill Companies *Financial Accounting*

Name _____ Date _____ Course _____ Section _____

Problem 1-6B

Assumption violated

1. _____

2. _____

3. _____

4. _____

Problem 1-7B

Terms	Definitions
1. _____ Predictive value	a. Decreases in equity resulting from transfers to owners.
2. _____ Relevance	b. Business transactions are measured using a common denominator.
3. _____ Timeliness	c. The indefinite life of a company can be broken into definite periods.
4. _____ Dividends	d. Information helps in understanding prior activities.
5. _____ Confirmatory value	e. Agreement between a measure and the phenomenon it represents.
6. _____ Faithful representation	f. Information arrives prior to the decision.
7. _____ Materiality	g. Information is related to the decision at hand.
8. _____ Monetary unit assumption	h. Information is useful in predicting the future.
9. _____ Periodicity assumption	i. Concerns the relative size of an item and its effect on decisions.

Name _____ **Date** _____ **Course** _____ **Section** _____

Exercise 2-1

	List A		List B
_____	1. Accounts	a.	Record of all transactions affecting a firm.
_____	2. Analyze transactions	b.	Determine the dual effect of economic events on the accounting equation.
_____	3. Journal	c.	List of accounts and their balances.
_____	4. Post	d.	Summary of the effects of all transactions related to a particular item over a period of time.
_____	5. Trail balance	e.	Transfer balances from the journal to the ledger

Exercise 2-2

	Assets	=	Liabilities	+	Stockholders' Equity
1.		=		+	
2.		=		+	
3.		=		+	
4.		=		+	
5.		=		+	
6.		=		+	

Exercise 2-3

Transactions	Dual Effect
(1) Issue 10,000 shares of common stock in exchange for $32,000 in cash.	
(2) Purchase land for $19,000. A note payable is signed for the full amount.	

The McGraw-Hill Companies *Financial Accounting*

Name _____ **Date** _____ **Course** _____ **Section** _____

Exercise 2-3 Continued

Transactions	Dual Effect
(3) Purchase storage container equipment for $8,000	
(4) Hire three employees for $2,000 per month.	
(5) Receive cash of $12,000 in rental fees for the current month.	
(6) Purchase office supplies for $2,000 on account.	
(7) Pay employees $6,000 for the first month's salaries.	

Exercise 2-4

Transactions	Dual Effect
(1) Paint houses in the current month for $15,000 on account.	
(2) Purchase painting equipment for $16,000 cash.	
(3) Purchase office supplies on account for $2,500.	
(4) Pay workers' salaries of $3,200 for the current month.	
(5) Purchase advertising to appear in the current month, $1200	
(6) Pay office rent of $4,400 for the current month.	
(7) Receive $10,000 from customers in (1) above.	
(8) Receive cash of $5,000 in advance from a customer that plans to have his house painted in the following month.	

Name _____ Date _____ Course _____ Section _____

Exercise 2-5

Transactions	Balance
Retained Earnings, April 1	_____
(1) Issue common stock for cash, $10,000.	_____
(2) Provide services to customers on account, $7,500.	_____
(3) Provide services to customers in exchange for cash, $2,200	_____
(4) Purchase equipment and pay cash, $6,600.	_____
(5) Pay rent for April, $1,200.	_____
(6) Pay workers' salaries for April, $2,500.	_____
(7) Pay dividends to stockholders, $1,500.	_____
Retained Earnings, April 30	_____

Exercise 2-6

Accounts	Debit or Credit
(1) Cash	_____
(2) Service Revenue	_____
(3) Salaries Expense	_____
(4) Accounts Payable	_____
(5) Equipment	_____
(6) Retained Earnings	_____
(7) Utilities Expense	_____
(8) Accounts Receivable	_____
(9) Dividends	_____
(10) Common Stock	_____

Name _____ Date _____ Course _____ Section _____

Exercise 2-7

Transactions	Account Debited	Account Credited
(1) Pay a cash dividend.		
(2) Pay rent in advance for the next three months.		
(3) Provide services to customers on account.		
(4) Purchase office supplies on account.		
(5) Pay salaries for the current month.		
(6) Issue common stock in exchange for cash.		
(7) Collect cash from customers for services provided in (3) above.		
(8) Borrow cash from the bank and sign a note.		
(9) Pay for the current month's utilities.		
(10) Pay for office supplies purchased in (4) above.		

Exercise 2-8

	Debit	Credit
(1) _____	_____	
_____		_____
_____		
(2) _____	_____	
_____		_____
_____		

         Financial Accounting

Name _____ Date _____ Course _____ Section _____

Exercise 2-8 Continued

	Debit	Credit
(3) _____	_____	
_____		_____
_____		
(4) _____	_____	
_____		_____
_____		
(5) _____	_____	
_____		_____
_____		

Exercise 2-9

(1) _____

(2) _____

(3) _____

(4) _____

(5) _____

Name _____ Date _____ Course _____ Section _____

Exercise 2-10

February 2   Debit   Credit

_____   _____

                    _____   _____

                    _____

February 7

_____   _____

                    _____   _____

                    _____

February 14

_____   _____

                    _____   _____

                    _____   _____

February 15

_____   _____

                    _____   _____

                    _____

February 25

_____   _____

                    _____   _____

                    _____

Name _____ Date _____ Course _____ Section _____

Exercise 2-10 Continued

February 28   **Debit**   **Credit**

_____   _____   _____

                    _____   _____   _____

                    _____

Exercise 2-11

March 1   **Debit**   **Credit**

_____

                    _____   _____   _____

                    _____

March 5

_____   _____

                    _____   _____   _____

                    _____

March 10

_____   _____

                    _____   _____   _____

                    _____   _____

March 15

_____   _____

                    _____   _____

                    _____   _____

Name _____ Date _____ Course _____ Section _____

Exercise 2-11 Continued

March 22		Debit	Credit
_____		_____	
	_____		_____
	_____		

March 27

_____		_____	
	_____		_____
	_____		_____

March 28

_____		_____	
	_____		_____
	_____		_____

Exercise 2-12

Cash	Accounts Receivable

Supplies	Account Payable

Name _____ Date _____ Course _____ Section _____

Exercise 2-12 Continued

Unearned Revenue

Service Revenue

Advertising Expense

Exercise 2-13

Sooner Company Trial Balance April 30		
Account Title	Debit	Credit
Totals		

Name _____ Date _____ Course _____ Section _____

Exercise 2-14

Fightin' Blue Hens Incorporated Trial Balance March 31		
Account Title	**Debit**	**Credit**
Totals		

Exercise 2-15

Requirement 1

	Debit	Credit

(1) _____   _____

_____   _____

_____   _____

(2) _____   _____

_____   _____

_____   _____

 Financial Accounting

Name _____ Date _____ Course _____ Section _____

Exercise 2-15 Continued

	Debit	Credit

(3) _____ _____

_____ _____

_____

(4) _____ _____

_____ _____

_____

(5) _____ _____

_____ _____

_____

_____

(6) _____ _____

_____ _____

_____

(7) _____ _____

_____ _____

_____

Name _____ Date _____ Course _____ Section _____

Exercise 2-15 Continued

Requirement 2

Cash		Common Stock

Land		Notes Payable

Equipment		Service Revenue

Supplies		Accounts Payable

Salaries Expense

The McGraw-Hill Companies   *Financial Accounting*

Name _____ Date _____ Course _____ Section _____

Exercise 2-15 Continued

Requirement 3

Golden Hurricane Company Trial Balance		
Account Title	Debit	Credit
Totals		

Exercise 2-16

Requirement 1   Debit   Credit

(1) _____   _____   _____

        _____   _____

        _____

(2) _____   _____   _____

        _____   _____

        _____

(3) _____   _____   _____

        _____   _____

        _____

Exercise 2-16 Continued

	Debit	Credit

(4) _____   _____   _____

_____   _____

_____   _____

(5) _____   _____   _____

_____   _____

_____   _____

(6) _____   _____   _____

_____   _____

_____   _____

(7) _____   _____   _____

_____   _____

_____   _____

(8) _____   _____   _____

_____   _____   _____

_____   _____

Name _____ Date _____ Course _____ Section _____

Exercise 2-16 Continued

Requirement 2

Account Receivables	Service Revenue

Equipment	Cash

Supplies	Account Payable

Salaries Expense	Advertising Expense

Rent Expense	Unearned Revenue

Name _____ Date _____ Course _____ Section _____

Exercise 2-16 Continued

Common Stock	Retained Earnings

Requirement 3

Boilermaker House Painting Company Trial Balance		
Account Title	**Debit**	**Credit**
Totals		

Problem 2-1A

Transaction	Assets	=	Liabilities	+	Stockholders' Equity
(1) Issue common stock in exchange for cash.		=		+	
(2) Purchase business supplies on account.		=		+	
(3) Pay for legal services for the current month.		=		+	
(4) Provide services to customers on account.		=		+	
(5) Pay employee salaries for the current month.		=		+	
(6) Provide services to customers for cash.		=		+	
(7) Pay for advertising for the current month.		=		+	
(8) Repay loan from the bank.		=		+	
(9) Pay dividends to stockholders.		=		+	
(10) Receive cash from customers in (4) above.		=		+	
(11) Pay for supplies purchased in (2) above.		=		+	

Problem 2-2A

Transaction	Assets	=	Liabilities	+	Stockholders' Equity
(1) Provide services to customers on account, $1,600.		=		+	
(2) Pay $400 for current month's rent.		=		+	
(3) Hire new employee, who will be paid $500 at the end of each month.		=		+	
(4) Pay $100 for advertising aired in the current period.		=		+	
(5) Purchase office supplies for cash.		=		+	
(6) Receive cash of $1,000 from customers in (1) above.		=		+	
(7) Obtain a loan from the bank for $7,000.		=		+	
(8) Receive a bill of $200 for utility costs in the current period.		=		+	
(9) Issue common stock for $10,000 cash.		=		+	
(10) Pay $500 to employee in (3) above.		=		+	
Totals		=		+	

2-18

Name _____ Date _____ Course _____ Section _____

Problem 2-3A

	Account Title	Type of Account	Normal Balance (Debit or Credit)
(1)	Salaries Payable		
(2)	Common Stock		
(3)	Prepaid Rent		
(4)	Buildings		
(5)	Utilities Expense		
(6)	Equipment		
(7)	Rent Expense		
(8)	Notes Payable		
(9)	Salaries Expense		
(10)	Insurance Expense		
(11)	Cash		
(12)	Service Revenue		

Problem 2-4A

External Transaction	Account Titles	Debit	Credit
1. Owners invest $10,000 in the company and receive common stock.			
2. Receive cash of $3,000 for services provided in the current period.			
3. Purchase office supplies on account, $200.			
4. Pay $500 for next month's rent.			
5. Purchase office equipment with cash of $1,700.			

The McGraw-Hill Companies *Financial Accounting*

Name _____ Date _____ Course _____ Section _____

Problem 2-5A

July 3		Debit	Credit

_____ _____

_____ _____

_____

July 6

_____ _____

_____ _____

_____

July 9

_____ _____

_____ _____

_____

July 14

_____ _____

_____ _____

_____

July 18

_____ _____

_____ _____

Name _____ Date _____ Course _____ Section _____

Problem 2-5A Continued

	Debit	Credit
<u>July 20</u>		
_____	_____	_____
_____		
<u>July 27</u>		
_____	_____	_____
_____		
<u>July 30</u>		
_____	_____	_____
_____		
<u>July 31</u>		
_____	_____	_____
_____		

Problem 2-6A

Requirement 1

	Debit	Credit
<u>July 3</u>		
_____	_____	_____
_____		

Name _____ Date _____ Course _____ Section _____

Problem 2-6A Continued

July 6   **Debit**   **Credit**

_____   _____

     _____   _____

     _____

July 9

_____   _____

     _____   _____

     _____

July 14

_____   _____

     _____   _____

     _____

July 18

_____   _____

     _____

     _____

July 20

_____   _____

     _____   _____

     _____

The McGraw-Hill Companies *Financial Accounting*

Name _____ Date _____ Course _____ Section _____

Problem 2-6A Continued

July 27		Debit	Credit
	_____	_____	_____
	_____	_____	_____
	_____		

July 30			
	_____	_____	_____
	_____	_____	_____
	_____		

July 31			
	_____	_____	_____
	_____	_____	_____
	_____		

Requirement 2

	Jake's Lawn Maintenance Company				Luke's Repair Shop			
	Assets	=	Liabilities	+	Stockholders' Equity	Assets	=	Liabilities	+	Stockholders' Equity
July 3		=		+			=		+	
July 6		=		+			=		+	
July 9		=		+			=		+	
July 14		=		+			=		+	
July 18		=		+			=		+	
July 20		=		+			=		+	
July 27		=		+			=		+	
July 30		=		+			=		+	
July 31		=		+			=		+	

 Financial Accounting

Name _____ Date _____ Course _____ Section _____

Problem 2-7A

Bruins Company Trial Balance November 30		
Account Title	**Debit**	**Credit**
Totals		

Name _____ Date _____ Course _____ Section _____

Problem 2-8A

Requirement 1

March 1   **Debit**   **Credit**

_____   _____

_____   _____

_____

March 3

_____   _____

_____   _____

_____

March 5

_____   _____

_____   _____

_____

March 7

_____   _____

_____   _____

_____

March 12

_____   _____

_____   _____

_____

The McGraw-Hill Companies   *Financial Accounting*

Name _____ Date _____ Course _____ Section _____

Problem 2-8A Continued

March 15   Debit   Credit

_____ _____ _____

_____ _____ _____

_____

March 19

_____ _____ _____

_____ _____ _____

_____

March 25

_____ _____ _____

_____ _____ _____

_____

March 30

_____ _____ _____

_____ _____ _____

_____

March 31

_____ _____ _____

_____ _____ _____

_____

Name _____ Date _____ Course _____ Section _____

Problem 2-8A Continued

Requirement 2 & 3

Cash	Supplies

Notes Payable	Accounts Payable

Utilities Expense	Rent Expense

Equipment	Dividends

Name _____ Date _____ Course _____ Section _____

Problem 2-8A Continued

Unearned Revenue

Service Revenue

Common Stock

Requirement 4

Ute Sewing Shop Trial Balance March 31		
Accounts	**Debit**	**Credit**
Total		

Name _____ Date _____ Course _____ Section _____

Problem 2-9A

Requirement 1

<u>Sep. 01</u>

	Debit	Credit
_____	_____	
_____		_____
_____		

<u>Sep. 02</u>

_____	_____	
_____		_____
_____		

<u>Sep. 04</u>

| _____ | _____ | |
| _____ | | |

<u>Sep. 08</u>

_____	_____	
_____		_____
_____		

<u>Sep. 10</u>

_____	_____	
_____		_____
_____		

Name _____ Date _____ Course _____ Section _____

Problem 2-9A Continued

Sep. 13	Debit	Credit

Sep. 18

Sep. 20

Sep. 30

Sep. 30

The McGraw-Hill Companies   *Financial Accounting*

2-30

Name _____ Date _____ Course _____ Section _____

Problem 2-9A Continued

Sep. 30		Debit	Credit

_____   _____

_____   _____

_____

Requirement 2 & 3

Cash

Accounts Receivable

Supplies

Accounts Payable

Utilities Expense

Rent Expense

Notes Payable

Dividends

The McGraw-Hill Companies

Financial Accounting

Name _____ Date _____ Course _____ Section _____

Problem 2-9A Continued

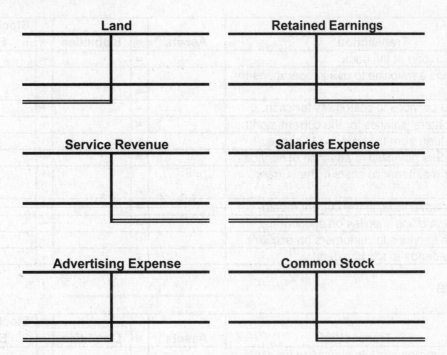

Land

Retained Earnings

Service Revenue

Salaries Expense

Advertising Expense

Common Stock

Requirement 4

Pirates Incorporated Trial Balance September 30		
Accounts	Debit	Credit
Totals		

       Financial Accounting

Problem 2-1B

	Transaction	Assets	=	Liabilities	+	Stockholders' Equity
(1)	Obtain a loan at the bank		=		+	
(2)	Purchase a machine to use in operations for cash.		=		+	
(3)	Provide services to customers for cash.		=		+	
(4)	Pay workers' salaries for the current month.		=		+	
(5)	Repay loan from the bank in (1) above.		=		+	
(6)	Customers pay cash in advance of services.		=		+	
(7)	Pay for maintenance costs in the current month.		=		+	
(8)	Pay for advertising in the current month.		=		+	
(9)	Purchase office supplies on account.		=		+	
(10)	Provide services to customers on account.		=		+	
(11)	Pay dividends to stockholders.		=		+	

Problem 2-2B

	Transaction	Assets	=	Liabilities	+	Stockholders' Equity
(1)	Issue common stock in exchange for cash, $15,000		=		+	
(2)	Obtain a loan from the bank for $9,000.		=		+	
(3)	Receive cash of $1,200 in advance from customers.		=		+	
(4)	Purchase supplies on account, $2,400.		=		+	
(5)	Pay one year of rent in advance, $12,000.		=		+	
(6)	Provide services to customers on account, $3,000.		=		+	
(7)	Repay $4,000 of the loan in (2) above.		=		+	
(8)	Pay the full amount for supplies purchased in (4) above.		=		+	
(9)	Provide services to customers in (3) above.		=		+	
(10)	Pay cash dividends of $1,000 to stockholders.		=		+	
	Totals		=		+	

Name _____ Date _____ Course _____ Section _____

Problem 2-3B

	Account Title		Type of Account	Normal Balance (Debit or Credit)
(1)	Supplies			
(2)	Advertising Expense			
(3)	Prepaid Insurance			
(4)	Supplies Expense			
(5)	Accounts Payable			
(6)	Equipment			
(7)	Dividends			
(8)	Accounts Receivable			
(9)	Retained Earnings			
(10)	Unearned Revenue			
(11)	Service Revenue			
(12)	Utilities Payable			

Problem 2-4B

External Transaction	Account Titles	Debit	Credit
1. Pay cash dividends of $700 to stockholders.			
2. Provide services on account for customers, $2,400.			
3. Pay a $400 utilities bill for the current period.			
4. Receive cash of $300 from previously billed customers.			
5. Pay for supplies previously purchased on account, $1,100.			

The McGraw-Hill Companies *Financial Accounting*

Name _____ Date _____ Course _____ Section _____

Problem 2-5B

May 2		Debit	Credit
_____		_____	
_____			_____
_____			

May 5

_____		_____	
_____			_____
_____			

May 7

_____		_____	
_____			_____
_____			

May 14

_____		_____	
_____			_____
_____			

May 19

_____		_____	
_____			_____
_____			

Problem 2-5B Continued

May 25		Debit	Credit
_____		_____	
_____			_____
_____			

May 28

_____		_____	
_____			_____
_____			

May 31

_____		_____	
_____			_____
_____			

Problem 2-6B

May 2		Debit	Credit
_____		_____	
_____			_____
_____			

May 5

_____		_____	
_____			_____
_____			

The McGraw-Hill Companies *Financial Accounting*

Name _____ Date _____ Course _____ Section _____

Problem 2-6B Continued

May 7		Debit	Credit
_____		_____	
_____			_____
_____			

May 14			
_____		_____	
_____			_____
_____			

May 19			
_____		_____	
_____			_____
_____			

May 25			
_____		_____	
_____			_____
_____			

May 28			
_____		_____	
_____			_____
_____			

 Financial Accounting

Name _____ Date _____ Course _____ Section _____

Problem 2-6B Continued

<u>May 31</u>   **Debit**   **Credit**

_____   _____

          _____   _____

          _____

	ELI'S TAX SERVICES				OLIVIA'S CLEANING SERVICES			
	Assets	=	Liabilities	+	Stockholders' Equity	Assets	=	Liabilities	+	Stockholders' Equity
May 5		=		+			=		+	
May 7		=		+			=		+	
May 14		=		+			=		+	
May 19		=		+			=		+	
May 25		=		+			=		+	
May 28		=		+			=		+	
May 31		=		+			=		+	

Problem 2-7B

DUCKS COMPANY		
Trial Balance		
September 30		
Account Title	Debit	Credit

Name _____ Date _____ Course _____ Section _____

Problem 2-7B Continued

Account Title	Debit	Credit
Totals		

Problem 2-8B

Requirement 1   Debit   Credit

June 1 ____

_____   _____

  _____   _____

    _____

June 2 ____

_____

  _____   _____

    _____

June 7 ____

_____   _____

  _____   _____

    _____

Name _____ **Date** _____ **Course** _____ **Section** _____

Problem 2-8B Continued

June 10		Debit	Credit

June 12

June 16

June 19

June 23

The McGraw-Hill Companies *Financial Accounting*

Name _____ Date _____ Course _____ Section _____

Problem 2-8B Continued

<u>June 29</u>   __Debit__   __Credit__

_____   _____

_____   _____

_____

<u>June 30</u>

_____   _____

_____   _____

_____

<u>June 30</u>

_____   _____

_____   _____

_____

Requirement 2 & 3

Cash	**Accounts Receivable**

Supplies	**Notes Payable**

Equipment	**Accounts Payable**

Name _____ Date _____ Course _____ Section _____

Problem 2-8B Continued

Common Stock		Dividends	

Service Revenue		Salaries Expense	

Advertising Expense		Utilities Expense	

Requirement 4

Salukis Car Cleaning Trial Balance June 30		
Account Title	**Debit**	**Credit**
Totals		

Name _____ Date _____ Course _____ Section _____

Problem 2-9B

Requirement 1

Nov. 1   Debit   Credit

_____ _____   _____ _____

         _____   _____ _____

Nov. 2

_____ _____   _____

         _____   _____ _____

         _____

Nov. 4

_____

         _____   _____ _____

Nov. 10

_____ _____   _____

         _____   _____ _____

         _____

Nov. 15

_____ _____   _____ _____

         _____   _____ _____

         _____

Name _____ Date _____ Course _____ Section _____

Problem 2-9B Continued

<u>Nov. 20</u>   Debit   Credit

_____   _____   _____

_____   _____   _____

_____   _____   _____

<u>Nov. 22</u>

_____   _____   _____

_____   _____   _____

_____   _____   _____

<u>Nov. 24</u>

_____   _____   _____

_____   _____   _____

_____   _____   _____

<u>Nov. 26</u>

_____   _____   _____

_____   _____   _____

_____   _____   _____

<u>Nov. 28</u>

_____   _____   _____

_____   _____   _____

_____   _____   _____

Name _____ Date _____ Course _____ Section _____

Problem 2-9B Continued

<u>Nov. 30</u>   **Debit**   **Credit**

_____   _____

_____   _____   _____

_____

Requirement 2 & 3

Cash	Accounts Receivable

Supplies	Equipment

Accounts Payable	Notes Payable

Common Stock	Retained Earnings

The McGraw-Hill Companies   *Financial Accounting*

Problem 2-9B Continued

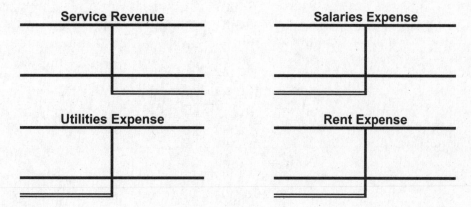

Service Revenue

Salaries Expense

Utilities Expense

Rent Expense

Requirement 4

Buckeye Incorporated Trial Balance November 30		
Account Title	Debit	Credit
Totals		

Name _____ Date _____ Course _____ Section _____

Exercise 3-1

1. **American Airlines** collects cash on June 12 from the sale of a ticket to a customer. The flight occurs on August 16. _____

2. A customer purchases sunglasses from **Eddie Bauer** on January 27 on account. Eddie Bauer receives payment from the customer on February 2. _____

3. On March 30, a customer preorders 10 supreme pizzas (without onions) from **Pizza Hut** for a birthday party. The pizzas are prepared and delivered on April 2. The company receives cash at the time of delivery. _____

4. A customer pays in advance for a three-month subscription to **Sports Illustrated** on July 1. Issues are scheduled for delivery each week from July 1 through September 30. _____

Exercise 3-2

1. **American Airlines** operates a flight from Dallas to Los Angeles on August 16. The pilots' salaries associated with the flight are paid on September 2. _____

2. **Eddie Bauer** pays cash on January 6 to purchase sunglasses from a wholesale distributor. The sunglasses are sold to customers on January 27. _____

3. On January 1, **Pizza Hut** pays for a one-year property insurance policy with coverage starting immediately. _____

4. **Sports Illustrated** signs an agreement with CBS on January 12 to provide television advertisements during the Super Bowl. Payment is due within 3 weeks after February 4, the day of the Super Bowl. Sports Illustrated makes the payment on February 23. _____

Name _____ Date _____ Course _____ Section _____

Exercise 3-3

1. **American Airlines** collects cash on June 12 from the sale of a ticket to a customer. The flight occurs on August 16. _____

2. A customer purchases sunglasses from **Eddie Bauer** on January 27 on account. Eddie Bauer receives payment from the customer on February 2. _____

3. On March 30, a customer preorders 10 supreme pizzas (without onions) from **Pizza Hut** for a birthday party. The pizzas are prepared and delivered on April 2. The company receives cash at the time of delivery. _____

4. A customer pays in advance for a three-month subscription to **Sports Illustrated** on July 1. Issues are scheduled for delivery each week from July 1 through September 30. _____

Exercise 3-4

1. **American Airlines** operates a flight from Dallas to Los Angeles on August 16. The pilots' salaries associated with the flight are paid on September 2. _____

2. **Eddie Bauer** pays cash on January 6 to purchase sunglasses from a wholesale distributor. The sunglasses are sold to customers on January 27. _____

3. On January 1, **Pizza Hut** pays for a one-year property insurance policy with coverage starting immediately. _____

4. **Sports Illustrated** signs an agreement with CBS on January 12 to provide television advertisements during the Super Bowl. Payment is due within 3 weeks after February 4, the day of the Super Bowl. Sports Illustrated makes the payment on February 23. _____

Name _____ Date _____ Course _____ Section _____

Exercise 3-5

Net income (unadjusted)	
a.	
b.	
c.	
d.	
Net income (adjusted)	

Exercise 3-6

_____ (a) Record and post adjusting entries.
_____ (b) Post the transaction to the T-account in the general ledger.
_____ (c) Record the transaction.
_____ (d) Prepare financial statements (income statement, statement of stockholders' equity, balance sheet, and statement of cash flows).
_____ (e) Record and post closing entries.
_____ (f) Prepare a trial balance.
_____ (g) Analyze the impact of the transaction on the accounting equation.
_____ (h) Assess whether the transaction results in a debit or a credit to the account balance.
_____ (i) Use source documents to identify accounts affected by external transactions.

Exercise 3-7

	Debit	Credit

(a) _____   _____

_____   _____

_____   _____

(b) _____   _____

_____   _____

_____   _____

(c) _____   _____

_____   _____

_____   _____

The McGraw-Hill Companies   *Financial Accounting*

3-4

Name _____ Date _____ Course _____ Section _____

Exercise 3-7 Continued

	Debit	Credit
(d) _____	_____	_____
_____	_____	_____
_____	_____	_____

Exercise 3-8

	Debit	Credit
(a) _____	_____	_____
_____	_____	_____
_____	_____	_____
(b) _____	_____	_____
_____	_____	_____
_____	_____	_____
(c) _____	_____	_____
_____	_____	_____
_____	_____	_____

Exercise 3-9

	Revenues	-	Expenses	=	Net Income
(a)		-		=	
(b)		-		=	
(c)					
	Total				

© 2011   The McGraw-Hill Companies   *Financial Accounting*

Name _____ Date _____ Course _____ Section _____

Exercise 3-10

		Debit	Credit
(a)	_____	_____	
	_____		_____
	_____		
(b)	_____	_____	
	_____		_____
	_____		
(c)	_____	_____	
	_____		_____
	_____		
(d)	_____	_____	
	_____		_____
	_____		

Exercise 3-11

	Assets	=	Liabilities	+	Stockholders' Equity
(a)		=		+	
(b)		=		+	
(c)		=		+	
(d)		=		+	
	Total				

Exercise 3-12

		Debit	Credit
(a)	_____	_____	_____
	_____		_____
	_____		
(b)	_____	_____	_____
	_____		_____
	_____		
(c)	_____	_____	_____
	_____		_____
	_____		
(d)	_____	_____	_____
	_____		_____
	_____		
(e)	_____	_____	_____

Exercise 3-13

		Debit	Credit
(a)	_____	_____	_____
	_____		_____
	_____		

Name _____ Date _____ Course _____ Section _____

Exercise 3-13 Continued

	Debit	Credit
(b) _____	_____	
_____		_____
_____		
(c) _____	_____	
_____		_____
_____		
(d) _____	_____	
_____		_____
_____		
(e) _____	_____	
_____		_____
_____		
_____		
(f) _____	_____	
_____		_____
_____		

Exercise 3-14

Requirement 1

	Debit	Credit
(a) _____	_____	
_____		_____
_____		

Exercise 3-14 Continued

	Debit	Credit
(b) _____	_____	_____
_____		_____
_____		
(c) _____	_____	_____
_____		_____
_____		
(d) _____	_____	_____
_____		_____
_____		

Requirement 2

Demon Deacons Corporation Adjusted Trial Balance		
Account Title	Debit	Credit
Totals		

Name _____ Date _____ Course _____ Section _____

Exercise 3-15

	VOLUNTEERS INC. (in millions)		RAIDERS INC. (in millions)	
Year	Net Income (Loss)	Retained Earnings	Net Income (Loss)	Retained Earnings
2003	_____	_____	_____	_____
2004	_____	_____	_____	_____
2005	_____	_____	_____	_____
2006	_____	_____	_____	_____
2007	_____	_____	_____	_____
2008	_____	_____	_____	_____
2009	_____	_____	_____	_____
2010	_____	_____	_____	_____
2011	_____	_____	_____	_____
2012	_____	_____	_____	_____

Exercise 3-16

Requirement 1

Blue Hens Corporation Income Statement For the year ended December 31, 2012		
Service revenue		
Total expenses		
Net income		

Name _____ Date _____ Course _____ Section _____

Exercise 3-16 Continued

Requirement 2

<table>
<tr><td colspan="4" align="center">Blue Hens Corporation
Balance Sheet
December 31, 2012</td></tr>
<tr><td align="center"><u>Assets</u></td><td></td><td align="center"><u>Liabilities</u></td><td></td></tr>
<tr><td></td><td></td><td></td><td></td></tr>
<tr><td></td><td></td><td></td><td></td></tr>
<tr><td></td><td></td><td></td><td></td></tr>
<tr><td></td><td></td><td></td><td></td></tr>
<tr><td></td><td></td><td></td><td></td></tr>
<tr><td></td><td></td><td align="center"><u>Stockholders' Equity</u></td><td></td></tr>
<tr><td></td><td></td><td></td><td></td></tr>
<tr><td></td><td></td><td></td><td></td></tr>
<tr><td>Total assets</td><td></td><td>Total liabilities and stockholders' equity</td><td></td></tr>
</table>

Exercise 3-17

<u>December 31, 2012</u>	**Debit**	**Credit**
_____	_____	
_____	_____	
	_____	_____
	_____	
_____	_____	
	_____	_____
	_____	_____
	_____	_____
	_____	
_____	_____	_____
	_____	_____

Exercise 3-18

December 31, 2012   Debit   Credit

_____   _____

_____   _____

_____   _____   _____

_____   _____

_____   _____

_____   _____

_____   _____

_____   _____   _____

_____   _____   _____

_____

Exercise 3-19

Requirement 1

December 31, 2012   Debit   Credit

_____   _____

_____   _____

_____   _____

_____   _____   _____

_____   _____

_____   _____

_____   _____

_____

Name _____ **Date** _____ **Course** _____ **Section** _____

Exercise 3-19 Continued

Requirement 2

Blue Hens Corporation Post-Closing Trial Balance December 31, 2012		
Account Title	**Debit**	**Credit**
Totals		

 Financial Accounting

Name _____ Date _____ Course _____ Section _____

Problem 3-1A

	Transaction	Accrual-basis		Cash-Basis	
		Revenue	Expense	Revenue	Expense
1.	Receive cash from customers in advance, $500				
2.	Pay utilities bill for the previous month, $100.				
3.	Pay for insurance one year in advance, $1,500				
4.	Pay workers' salaries for the current month, $700.				
5.	Record depreciation of building, $900.				
6.	Receive cash from customers at the time of service, $1,200				
7.	Purchase office supplies on account, $230.				
8.	Borrow cash from the bank, $3,000.				
9.	Receive cash from customers for services performed last month, $650.				
10.	Pay for advertising to appear in the current month, $350.				

Problem 3-2A

Minutemen Law Services Income Statement For the year ended December 31, 2012		
Net income		

 Financial Accounting

Name _____ Date _____ Course _____ Section _____

Problem 3-3A

		Debit	Credit

(a) _____ _____

_____ _____

_____

(b) _____ _____

_____ _____

_____

(c) _____ _____

_____ _____

_____

(d) _____ _____

_____ _____

_____ _____

(e) _____ _____

_____ _____

_____

Problem 3-4A

		Debit	Credit

(a) _____ _____

_____ _____

_____

(b) _____ _____

_____ _____

_____

Name _____ Date _____ Course _____ Section _____

Problem 3-4A Continued

		Debit	Credit
(c) _____	_____	_____	_____
	_____	_____	_____
	_____		
(d) _____	_____	_____	_____
	_____	_____	_____
	_____		
(e) _____	_____	_____	_____
	_____	_____	_____
	_____		
(f) _____	_____	_____	_____
	_____		

The McGraw-Hill Companies *Financial Accounting*

Problem 3-5A

Boilermaker Unlimited Income Statement For the year ended December 31, 2012		
Net income		

Boilermaker Unlimited Statement of Stockholders' Equity For the year ended December 31, 2012			
	Common Stock	Retained Earnings	Total Stockholders' Equity
Balance at January 1			
Balance at December 31			

Name _____ Date _____ Course _____ Section _____

Problem 3-5A Continued

Assets		Liabilities	
		Total current liabilities	
Total current assets			
		Stockholders' Equity	
		Total stockholders' equity	
Total assets		Total liabilities and stockholders' equity	

Boilermaker Unlimited
Balance Sheet
December 31, 2012

Problem 3-6A

Requirement 1

<u>December 31, 2012</u>   Debit   Credit

_____   _____   _____

                                        _____   _____

                                        _____

_____   _____

                                        _____   _____

                                        _____

                                        _____

                                        _____

_____   _____

_____   _____

                                        _____

Name _____ Date _____ Course _____ Section _____

Problem 3-6A Continued

Requirement 2

Blue Devil Tax Services		
Post-Closing Trial Balance		
Account	Debit	Credit
Totals		

Problem 3-7A

Requirement 1 and 2

Cash   Accounts Receivable   Supplies

Prepaid Rent   Equipment   Accumulated Depr.

Accounts Payable   Salaries Payable   Interest Payable

Utilities Payable   Notes Payable   Common Stock

Name _____ Date _____ Course _____ Section _____

Problem 3-7A Continued

Retained Earnings	Service Revenue	Salaries Expense

Interest Expense	Rent Expense	Supplies Expense

Utilities Expense	Depr. Expense

Requirement 3

Crimson Tide Music Academy Adjusted Trial Balance December 31, 2012		
Account Title	**Debit**	**Credit**
Totals		

Name _____ Date _____ Course _____ Section _____

Problem 3-7A Continued

Requirement 4

Crimson Tide Music Academy Income Statement For the year ended December 31, 2012		
Net income		

Crimson Tide Music Academy Statement of Stockholders' Equity For the year ended December 31, 2012	Common Stock	Retained Earnings	Total Stockholders' Equity
Balance at January 1			
Balance at December 31			

Crimson Tide Music Academy Balance Sheet December 31, 2012			
Assets		**Liabilities**	
Total current assets		Total current liabilities	
		Stockholders' Equity	
		Total stockholders' equity	
Total assets		Total liabilities and stockholders' equity	

 Financial Accounting

Name _____ Date _____ Course _____ Section _____

Problem 3-7A Continued

Requirement 5

	Debit	Credit
_____	_____	
_____		_____
_____		
_____	_____	
_____		_____
_____		_____
_____		_____
_____		_____
_____		_____
_____		_____
_____		_____
_____		

Requirement 6

Retained Earnings	Service Revenue	Salaries Expense
Interest Expense	Rent Expense	Supplies Expense
Utilities Expense	Depr. Expense	

Name _____ Date _____ Course _____ Section _____

Problem 3-7A Continued

Requirement 7

Crimson Tide Music Academy Post-Closing Trial Balance December 31, 2012		
Account Title	**Debit**	**Credit**
Total		

Problem 3-8A

Requirement 1

Cash	Accounts Receivable	Supplies

Equipment	Accumulated Depr.	Salaries Payable

Common Stock	Retained Earnings	Service Revenue

Name _____ Date _____ Course _____ Section _____

Problem 3-8A Continued

Dividends	Salaries Expense	R&M Expense

Depr. Expense	Supplies Expense

Requirement 2

	Debit	Credit

(a) _____

_____

_____

_____

(b) _____

_____

_____

(c) _____

_____

_____

(d) _____

_____

_____

_____

The McGraw-Hill Companies *Financial Accounting*

Name _____ Date _____ Course _____ Section _____

Problem 3-8A Continued

	Debit	Credit
(e) _____	_____	_____
_____		_____
_____		
(f) _____	_____	
_____		_____
_____		
(g) _____	_____	
_____		_____
_____		

Requirement 3

Cash	Accounts Receivable	Supplies

Equipment	Accumulated Depr.	Salaries Payable

Common Stock	Retained Earnings	Service Revenue

The McGraw-Hill Companies *Financial Accounting*

Name _____ Date _____ Course _____ Section _____

Problem 3-8A Continued

Dividends	Salaries Expense	R&M Expense

Depr. Expense	Supplies Expense

Requirement 4

Red Storm Cleaners Unadjusted Trial Balance December 31, 2012		
Account Title	Debit	Credit
Total		

The McGraw-Hill Companies *Financial Accounting*

Name _____ **Date** _____ **Course** _____ **Section** _____

Problem 3-8A Continued

Requirement 5

	Debit	Credit
_____	_____	
_____		_____
_____		
_____	_____	
_____		
_____	_____	
_____		_____
_____		

Requirement 6

Cash	Accounts Receivable	Supplies

Equipment	Accumulated Depr.	Salaries Payable

Name _____ Date _____ Course _____ Section _____

Problem 3-8A Continued

Common Stock	Retained Earnings	Service Revenue

Dividends	Salaries Expense	R&M Expense

Depr. Expense	Supplies Expense

Requirement 7

Red Storm Cleaners
Adjusted Trial Balance
December 31, 2012

Account Title	Debit	Credit
Total		

 Financial Accounting

Name _____ Date _____ Course _____ Section _____

Problem 3-8A Continued

Requirement 8

Red Storm Cleaners Income Statement For the year ended December 31, 2012		
Net Income		

Red Storm Cleaners Balance Sheet December 31, 2012			
Assets		**Liabilities**	
Total current assets			
		Stockholders' Equity	
		Total stockholders' equity	
Total assets		Total liabilities and stockholders'	

Requirement 9

<u>December 31, 2012</u>   **Debit**   **Credit**

_____   _____

          _____   _____

          _____

The McGraw-Hill Companies   *Financial Accounting*

Name _____ Date _____ Course _____ Section _____

Problem 3-8A Continued

<u>December 31, 2012</u>   **Debit**   **Credit**

_____   _____

         _____   _____

         _____   _____

         _____   _____

         _____

_____   _____

         _____   _____

         _____

Requirement 10

Cash	Accounts Receivable	Supplies

Equipment	Accumulated Depr.	Salaries Payable

Common Stock	Retained Earnings	Service Revenue

     The McGraw-Hill Companies   *Financial Accounting*

Name _____ Date _____ Course _____ Section _____

Problem 3-8A Continued

Dividends	Salaries Expense	R&M Expense

Depr. Expense	Supplies Expense

Requirement 11

Red Storm Cleaners Post-Closing Trial Balance December 31, 2012		
Account Title	**Debit**	**Credit**
Total		

Name _____ Date _____ Course _____ Section _____

Problem 3-1B

	Transaction	Accrual-basis		Cash-Basis	
		Revenue	Expense	Revenue	Expense
1.	Receive cash from customers at the time of service, $2,700.				
2.	Issue common stock for cash, $5,000.				
3.	Receive cash from customers who were previously billed, $1,200.				
4.	Record depreciation of equipment, $500.				
5.	Pay workers' salaries for the current month, $600.				
6.	Pay for rent one year in advance, $2,400.				
7.	Repay a long-term note to the bank, $2,000.				
8.	Pay workers' salaries for the previous month, $750.				
9.	Pay dividends to stockholders, $400.				
10.	Purchase office supplies for cash, $440.				

Problem 3-2B

Horned Frogs Fine Cooking Income Statement For the year ended December 31, 2012		
Net income		

Name _____ Date _____ Course _____ Section _____

Problem 3-3B

		Debit	Credit
(a)	_____	_____	
	_____		
	_____		
(b)	_____	_____	
	_____		
	_____		
(c)	_____	_____	
	_____		_____
	_____		
(d)	_____	_____	
	_____		
	_____		
(e)	_____	_____	
	_____	_____	_____
	_____		
(f)	_____	_____	
	_____	_____	_____
	_____		
(g)	_____	_____	_____
	_____		_____
	_____		

The McGraw-Hill Companies *Financial Accounting*

Name _____ Date _____ Course _____ Section _____

Problem 3-4B

	Debit	Credit
(a) _____	_____	_____
_____	_____	_____
(b) _____	_____	_____
_____	_____	_____
(c) _____	_____	_____
_____	_____	_____
(d) _____	_____	_____
_____	_____	_____
(e) _____	_____	_____
_____	_____	_____
(f) _____	_____	_____
_____	_____	_____
_____	_____	_____

The McGraw-Hill Companies   *Financial Accounting*

Name _____ **Date** _____ **Course** _____ **Section** _____

Problem 3-5B

Orange Designs Income Statement For the year ended December 31, 2012		
Net income		

Orange Designs Statement of Stockholders' Equity For the year ended December 31, 2012			
	Common Stock	Retained Earnings	Total Stockholders' Equity
Balance at January 1			
Balance at December 31			

Name _____ **Date** _____ **Course** _____ **Section** _____

Problem 3-5B Continued

Assets		Liabilities	
		Total current liabilities	
Total current assets			
		Stockholders' Equity	
		Total stockholders' equity	
		Total liabilities and stockholders'	

Table title:
Orange Designs
Balance Sheet
December 31, 2012

Problem 3-6B

Requirement 1

December 31, 2012	Debit	Credit

Name _____ Date _____ Course _____ Section _____

Problem 3-6B Continued

Requirement 2

Fighting Illini Post-Closing Trial Balance		
Account	Debit	Credit
Totals		

Problem 3-7B

Requirement 1 and 2

Cash	Accounts Receivable	Supplies

Prepaid Insurance	Equipment	Accumulated Depr.

Accounts Payable	Salaries Payable	Utilities Payable

Interest Payable	Notes Payable	Common Stock

Name _____ Date _____ Course _____ Section _____

Problem 3-7B Continued

Retained Earnings	Dividends	Service Revenue

Salaries Expense	Depreciation Expense	Insurance Expense

Supplies Expense	Utilities Expense	Interest Expense

Requirement 3

Jaguar Auto Company
Adjusted Trial Balance
December 31, 2012

Account Title	Debit	Credit
Totals		

Name _____ Date _____ Course _____ Section _____

Problem 3-7B Continued

Requirement 4

Jaguar Auto Company Income Statement For the year ended December 31, 2012		
Net income		

Jaguar Auto Company Statement of Stockholders' Equity For the year ended December 31, 2012			
	Common Stock	Retained Earnings	Total Stockholders' Equity
Balance at January 1			
Balance at December 31			

Jaguar Auto Company Balance Sheet December 31, 2012			
Assets		**Liabilities**	
Total current assets		Total current liabilities	
		Stockholders' Equity	
		Total stockholders' equity	
Total assets		Total liabilities and stockholders' equity	

Name _____ Date _____ Course _____ Section _____

Problem 3-7B Continued

Requirement 5

	Debit	Credit

Requirement 6

Retained Earnings	Dividends	Service Revenue

Salaries Expense	Depreciation Expense	Insurance Expense

Supplies Expense	Utilities Expense	Interest Expense

Name _____ Date _____ Course _____ Section _____

Problem 3-7B Continued

Requirement 7

Jaguar Auto Company Post-Closing Trial Balance December 31, 2012		
Account Title	Debit	Credit
Total		

Problem 3-8B

Requirement 1

Cash	Accounts Receivable	Supplies

Equipment	Accumulated Depr.	Accounts Payable

Utilities Payable	Unearned Revenue	Common Stock

Name _____ Date _____ Course _____ Section _____

Problem 3-8B Continued

Retained Earnings	Dividends	Service Revenue

Salaries Expense	Utilities Expense	Supplies Expense

Depr. Expense

Requirement 2

	Debit	Credit
(a)		
(b)		
(c)		
(d)		

The McGraw-Hill Companies *Financial Accounting*

Name _____ Date _____ Course _____ Section _____

Problem 3-8B Continued

	Debit	Credit
(e) _____	_____	_____
_____		
		_____
_____		
(f) _____	_____	
_____		_____
_____		
(g) _____		_____
_____		
_____		_____

Requirement 3

Cash	Accounts Receivable	Supplies

Equipment	Accumulated Depr.	Accounts Payable

Utilities Payable	Unearned Revenue	Common Stock

Name _____ Date _____ Course _____ Section _____

Problem 3-8B Continued

Retained Earnings	Dividends	Service Revenue

Salaries Expense	Utilities Expense	Supplies Expense

Depr. Expense

Requirement 4

Pipers Plumbing		
Unadjusted Trial Balance		
December 31, 2012		
Account Title	Debit	Credit
Total		

Financial Accounting

Name _____ Date _____ Course _____ Section _____

Problem 3-8B Continued

Requirement 5

	Debit	Credit
_____	_____	
_____		_____
_____		
_____		_____
_____	_____	
_____		
_____	_____	
_____		
_____		

Requirement 6

Cash	Accounts Receivable	Supplies

Equipment	Accumulated Depr.	Accounts Payable

Utilities Payable	Unearned Revenue	Common Stock

Name _____ Date _____ Course _____ Section _____

Problem 3-8B Continued

Retained Earnings	Dividends	Service Revenue

Salaries Expense	Utilities Expense	Supplies Expense

Depr. Expense

Requirement 7

Pipers Plumbing Adjusted Trial Balance December 31, 2012		
Account Title	**Debit**	**Credit**
Total		

The McGraw-Hill Companies *Financial Accounting*

Name _____ **Date** _____ **Course** _____ **Section** _____

Problem 3-8B Continued

Requirement 8

Pipers Plumbing Income Statement For the year ended December 31, 2012		
Net Income		

Pipers Plumbing Balance Sheet December 31, 2012			
Assets		**Liabilities**	
Total current assets			
		Stockholders' Equity	
		Total stockholders' equity	
Total assets		Total liabilities and stockholders'	

Requirement 9

<u>December 31, 2012</u>   **Debit**   **Credit**

_____   _____

_____   _____

_____

Name _____ Date _____ Course _____ Section _____

Problem 3-8B Continued

<u>December 31, 2012</u>   Debit   Credit

_____ _____   _____

                          _____   _____
                          _____   _____
                          _____   _____

                          _____   _____

                          _____   _____

                          _____   _____

Requirement 10

Cash	Accounts Receivable	Supplies

Equipment	Accumulated Depr.	Accounts Payable

Utilities Payable	Unearned Revenue	Common Stock

Name _____ Date _____ Course _____ Section _____

Problem 3-8B Continued

Retained Earnings	Dividends	Service Revenue

Salaries Expense	Utilities Expense	Supplies Expense

Depr. Expense

Requirement 11

Pipers Plumbing Post-Closing Trial Balance December 31, 2012		
Account Title	**Debit**	**Credit**
Total		

Name _____ **Date** _____ **Course** _____ **Section** _____

Exercise 4-1

1.	
2.	
3.	
4.	
5.	
6.	

Exercise 4-2

1.	
2.	
3.	
4.	
5.	
6.	

Exercise 4-3

1.	
2.	
3.	
4.	
5.	
6.	
7.	
8.	
9.	

Exercise 4-4

1.	
2.	
3.	
4.	
5.	
6.	

The McGraw-Hill Companies *Financial Accounting*

Name _____ Date _____ Course _____ Section _____

Exercise 4-5

Total Cash	

Exercise 4-6

_____

_____

_____

_____

_____

Exercise 4-7

_____

_____

_____

_____

_____

Exercise 4-8

_____

_____

Exercise 4-9

Reconciled bank balance	

Name _____ **Date** _____ **Course** _____ **Section** _____

Exercise 4-10

Reconciled company balance	

Exercise 4-11

	Debit	Credit

Exercise 4-12

Spielberg Company Bank Reconciliation July 31, 2012			
Bank's Cash Balance		**Company's Cash Balance**	
Before reconciliation		Before reconciliation	
After reconciliation		After reconciliation	

Exercise 4-13

The Dean Acting Academy Bank Reconciliation August 31, 2012			
Bank's Cash Balance		**Company's Cash Balance**	
Before reconciliation		Before reconciliation	
After reconciliation		After reconciliation	

Exercise 4-14

September 4	Debit	Credit
_____	_____	
_____		_____
_____		

September 30		
_____		
_____		
_____		
_____		_____
_____		

September 30		
_____		_____
_____		
_____		_____

Name _____ Date _____ Course _____ Section _____

Exercise 4-15

April 3   Debit   Credit

_____   _____   _____

                    _____   _____

                    _____   _____

April 30

_____   _____   _____

_____   _____   _____

_____   _____   _____

_____   _____   _____

                    _____   _____

                    _____   _____

April 30

_____   _____   _____

                    _____   _____

                    _____   _____

Name _____ Date _____ Course _____ Section _____

Exercise 4-16

Transaction	Cash involved? (yes or no)	If yes, is it operating, investing, or financing?	Inflow or Outflow?
a. Borrow cash from the bank.			
b. Purchase supplies on account.			
c. Purchase equipment with cash.			
d. Sell merchandise on account.			
e. Pay cash on account for #2 above.			
f. Sell for cash a warehouse no longer in use.			
g. Receive cash on account for #4 above.			
h. Pay cash to workers for wages.			

Exercise 4-17

Requirement 1 and 2

Transaction	Inflow or Outflow of cash?	Operating, investing, or financing?
a. Issue common stock for cash, $50,000.		
b. Purchase building and land with cash, $35,000.		
c. Provide services to customers on account, $7,000.		
d. Pay utilities on building, $1,000.		
e. Collect $5,000 on account from customers.		
f. Pay employee wages, $9,000.		
g. Pay dividends to stockholders $4,000.		
Net cash flows for the year		

Exercise 4-17 Continued

Requirement 3

_____

_____

Exercise 4-18

a. Cash used for purchase of office supplies   _____
b. Cash provide from consulting to customers   _____
c. Cash used for purchase of mining equipment   _____
d. Cash provided from long-term borrowing   _____
e. Cash used for payment of employee salaries   _____
f. Cash used for payment of office rent   _____
g. Cash provided from sale of equipment purchased in
   c. above   _____
h. Cash used to repay a portion of the long-term
   borrowing in d. above   _____
i. Cash used to pay office utilities   _____
j. Purchase of company vehicle   _____
Cash flows from operating activities   =========

Exercise 4-19

a. Cash used for purchase of office supplies   _____
b. Cash provide from consulting to customers   _____
c. Cash used for purchase of mining equipment   _____
d. Cash provided from long-term borrowing   _____
e. Cash used for payment of employee salaries   _____
f. Cash used for payment of office rent   _____
g. Cash provided from sale of equipment purchased in
   c. above   _____
h. Cash used to repay a portion of the long-term
   borrowing in d. above   _____
i. Cash used to pay office utilities   _____
j. Purchase of company vehicle   _____
Cash flows from investing activities   =========

Name _____ Date _____ Course _____ Section _____

Exercise 4-20

a. Cash used for purchase of office supplies _____
b. Cash provide from consulting to customers _____
c. Cash used for purchase of mining equipment _____
d. Cash provided from long-term borrowing _____
e. Cash used for payment of employee salaries _____
f. Cash used for payment of office rent _____
g. Cash provided from sale of equipment purchased in c. above _____
h. Cash used to repay a portion of the long-term borrowing in d. above _____
i. Cash used to pay office utilities _____
j. Purchase of company vehicle _____
Cash flows from financing activities _____

Exercise 4-21

_____
_____
_____
_____
_____
_____
_____
_____
_____
_____
_____
_____

Name _____ Date _____ Course _____ Section _____

Problem 4-1A

Requirement 1

_____

_____

_____

_____

_____

_____

_____

_____

_____

_____

Requirement 2

_____

_____

_____

_____

_____

_____

_____

_____

_____

_____

Requirement 3 and 4

_____

_____

_____

_____

_____

_____

_____

_____

_____

_____

_____

_____

_____

Name _____ Date _____ Course _____ Section _____

Problem 4-2A

Requirement 1

Oscar's Red Carpet Store Bank Reconciliation February 28, 2012			
Bank's Cash Balance		**Company's** Cash Balance	
Before reconciliation		Before reconciliation	
After reconciliation		After reconciliation	

Requirement 2

	Debit	Credit

Name _____ Date _____ Course _____ Section _____

Problem 4-3A

Requirement 1

Diaz Entertainment Bank Reconciliation May 31, 2012			
Bank's Cash Balance		**Company's** Cash Balance	
Before reconciliation		Before reconciliation	
After reconciliation		After reconciliation	

Requirement 2

	Debit	Credit

Name _____ Date _____ Course _____ Section _____

Problem 4-4A

Pixar Toy Manufacturing Statement of Cash Flows For the month ended August 31, 2012		
Cash Flows from Operating Activities		
Net cash flows from operating activities		
Cash Flows from Investing Activities		
Net cash flows from investing activities		
Cash Flows from Financing Activities		
Net cash flows from financing activities		
Cash at the end of the month		

 Financial Accounting

Name _____ Date _____ Course _____ Section _____

Problem 4-5A

Requirement 1

October 2

	Debit	Credit

_____

    _____ _____ _____

    _____

October 5

_____ _____

    _____ _____

    _____

October 9

_____ _____

    _____ _____

    _____ _____

    _____

October 12

_____ _____

    _____ _____

    _____

October 19

_____ _____

    _____ _____

    _____

Name _____ **Date** _____ **Course** _____ **Section** _____

Problem 4-5A Continued

<u>October 22</u>   **Debit**   **Credit**

_____   _____   _____

   _____   _____

   _____

<u>October 25</u>

_____   _____

   _____   _____

   _____

<u>October 30</u>

_____   _____

   _____   _____

   _____

<u>October 31</u>

_____   _____

   _____   _____

   _____

Requirement 2

_____
_____
_____
_____
_____

Name _____ Date _____ Course _____ Section _____

Problem 4-5A Continued

Requirement 3

Cash

Requirement 4

Balboa's Gym Statement of Cash Flows For the month ended October 31		
Cash Flows from Operating Activities		
Net cash flows from operating activities		
Cash Flows from Investing Activities		
Net cash flows from investing activities		
Cash Flows from Financing Activities		
Net cash flows from financing activities		
Cash at the end of the month		

Requirement 5

_____

_____

_____

Name _____ Date _____ Course _____ Section _____

Problem 4-1B

Requirement 1

Howard Productions Bank Reconciliation February 28			
Bank's Cash Balance		**Company's** Cash Balance	
Before reconciliation		Before reconciliation	
After reconciliation		After reconciliation	

Requirement 2

_____
_____
_____
_____
_____
_____
_____
_____
_____
_____
_____
_____
_____
_____
_____

Problem 4-2B

Requirement 1

Blockwood Video Bank Reconciliation October 31, 2012			
Bank's Cash Balance		**Company's** Cash Balance	
Before reconciliation		Before reconciliation	
After reconciliation		After reconciliation	

Name _____ Date _____ Course _____ Section _____

Problem 4-2B Continued

Requirement 2

	Debit	Credit
_____	_____	
_____		_____
_____		_____
_____	_____	
_____	_____	
_____	_____	
_____	_____	
_____		_____

Problem 4-3B

Requirement 1

Glover Incorporated Bank Reconciliation July 31, 2012			
Bank's Cash Balance		**Company's Cash Balance**	
Before reconciliation		Before reconciliation	
After reconciliation		After reconciliation	

Requirement 2

	Debit	Credit
_____	_____	
_____		_____
_____		_____

The McGraw-Hill Companies *Financial Accounting*

Name _____ Date _____ Course _____ Section _____

Problem 4-3B Continued

	Debit	Credit
_____	_____	
_____	_____	
_____	_____	
_____	_____	
_____		_____
_____		

Problem 4-4B

Requirement 1

Dreamworks Bedding Supplies Statement of Cash Flows For the month ended August 31, 2012		
Cash Flows from Operating Activities		
Net cash flows from operating activities		
Cash Flows from Investing Activities		
Net cash flows from investing activities		
Cash Flows from Financing Activities		
Net cash flows from financing activities		
Cash at the end of the month		

Name _____ Date _____ Course _____ Section _____

Problem 4-5B

Requirement 1

June 2   **Debit**   **Credit**

_____   _____

      _____   _____

      _____

June 3

_____   _____

      _____   _____

      _____

June 7

_____   _____
_____   _____

      _____   _____

      _____

June 11

_____   _____

      _____   _____

      _____

June 17

_____   _____

      _____   _____

      _____

Name _____ Date _____ Course _____ Section _____

Problem 4-5B Continued

<u>June 22</u>   Debit   Credit

_____   _____   _____

       _____   _____

       _____

<u>June 25</u>

_____   _____

       _____   _____

       _____

<u>June 28</u>

_____   _____

       _____   _____

       _____

<u>June 30</u>

_____   _____

       _____   _____

       _____

Requirement 2

_____
_____
_____
_____
_____
_____
_____

Name _____ Date _____ Course _____ Section _____

Problem 4-5B Continued

Requirement 3

Cash

Requirement 4

Web Slinger Pet Shop Statement of Cash Flows For the month ended June 30		
Cash Flows from Operating Activities		
Net cash flows from operating activities		
Cash Flows from Investing Activities		
Net cash flows from investing activities		
Cash Flows from Financing Activities		
Net cash flows from financing activities		
Cash at the end of the month		

Requirement 5

_____
_____
_____
_____
_____
_____

The McGraw-Hill Companies *Financial Accounting*

Name _____ Date _____ Course _____ Section _____

Exercise 5-1

May 7   **Debit**   **Credit**

_____   _____

                    _____   _____   _____

                    _____

May 13

_____   _____

                    _____   _____   _____

                    _____   _____

Exercise 5-2

May 1   **Debit**   **Credit**

_____   _____

                    _____   _____   _____

                    _____

Exercise 5-3

March 12   **Debit**   **Credit**

_____   _____

                    _____   _____   _____

                    _____

March 20

_____   _____

_____   _____

                    _____   _____   _____

                    _____

The McGraw-Hill Companies   *Financial Accounting*

Name _____ Date _____ Course _____ Section _____

Exercise 5-4

<u>March 12</u>   Debit   Credit

_____   _____

                 _____   _____

                 _____

<u>March 31</u>

_____   _____

                 _____   _____

                 _____

Exercise 5-5

<u>March 12</u>   Debit   Credit

_____   _____

                 _____   _____

                 _____

<u>March 31</u>

_____   _____

                 _____   _____

                 _____

Name _____ Date _____ Course _____ Section _____

Exercise 5-6

Requirement 1

<u>April 25</u>   Debit _____   Credit _____

_____   _____

                    _____   _____

                    _____

Requirement 2

<u>April 27</u>   Debit _____   Credit _____

_____   _____

                    _____   _____

                    _____

Requirement 3

<u>April 30</u>   Debit _____   Credit _____

_____   _____

                    _____   _____

                    _____

Requirement 4

Net sales	

Exercise 5-7

Requirement 1

December 31, 2012	Debit	Credit
_____	_____	_____
_____	_____	_____
_____		

Requirement 2

Net realizable value	

Exercise 5-8

Requirement 1

December 31, 2012	Debit	Credit
_____	_____	_____
_____	_____	_____
_____		

Requirement 2

Bad debt Expense	
Allowance for uncollectible accounts	

Requirement 3

Net realizable value	

Name _____ Date _____ Course _____ Section _____

Exercise 5-9

Requirement 1

<u>December 31, 2010</u>   **Debit**   **Credit**

_____   _____

                          _____   _____

                          _____

Requirement 2

Bad debt Expense	
Allowance for uncollectible accounts	

Requirement 3

Net realizable value	

Exercise 5-10

Credit sales transaction cycle	Assets	Liabilities	Stockholders' equity	Revenues	Expenses
1. Provide services on account					
2. Estimate uncollectible accounts					
3. Write off accounts as uncollectible					
4. Collect on account previously written off					

Exercise 5-11

Requirement 1

Age Group	Amount Receivable	Estimated Percent Uncollectible	Estimated Amount Uncollectible
Not yet due			
0-30 days past due			
31-90 days past due			
More than 90 days past due			
Total			

Name _____ Date _____ Course _____ Section _____

Exercise 5-11 Continued

Requirement 2

<u>December 31, 2010</u>   Debit   Credit

_____ _____

        _____   _____

        _____

Requirement 3

Net realizable value	

Exercise 5-12

Requirement 1

Age Group	Amount Receivable	Estimated Percent Uncollectible	Estimated Amount Uncollectible
Not yet due			
0-60 days past due			_____
61-120 days past due			_____
More than 120 days past due	_____		_____
Total			

Requirement 2

<u>December 31, 2010</u>   Debit   Credit

_____ _____

        _____   _____

Requirement 3

Net realizable value	

Name _____ Date _____ Course _____ Section _____

Exercise 5-13

Requirement 1

	Debit	Credit
a. _____	_____	_____
_____	_____	_____
_____		
b. _____	_____	_____
_____	_____	_____
c. _____	_____	_____
_____	_____	_____
d. _____	_____	_____
_____	_____	_____
_____		

Requirement 2

	Debit	Credit
a. _____	_____	_____
_____		_____
_____		
b. _____	_____	_____
_____		_____
_____		

Name _____ **Date** _____ **Course** _____ **Section** _____

Exercise 5-13 Continued

	Debit	Credit
c. _____	_____	_____
_____	_____	_____
_____		
d. _____	_____	_____
_____	_____	_____
_____		

Requirement 3

Bad Debt Expense	Allowance Method	Direct Write-off Method
2012 :	_____	_____
2013 :	_____	_____

_____
_____
_____
_____
_____
_____
_____
_____

Exercise 5-14

April 11

	Debit	Credit
_____	_____	_____
_____		_____
_____		

_____

The McGraw-Hill Companies *Financial Accounting*

Name _____ Date _____ Course _____ Section _____

Exercise 5-14 Continued

<u>June 1</u>   **Debit**   **Credit**

_____   _____

     _____   _____

     _____

<u>November 1</u>

_____

     _____   _____

     _____

Exercise 5-15

<u>March 1</u>   **Debit**   **Credit**

_____   _____

     _____   _____

     _____

<u>September 1</u>

_____   _____

     _____   _____

     _____

Exercise 5-16

<u>March 1</u>   **Debit**   **Credit**

_____   _____

     _____   _____

     _____

     The McGraw-Hill Companies   *Financial Accounting*

Exercise 5-16 Continued

September 1   **Debit**   **Credit**

_____   _____

_____   _____

           _____   _____

           _____

Exercise 5-17

Requirement 1

April 1, 2012   **Debit**   **Credit**

_____   _____

           _____   _____

           _____

Requirement 2

December 31, 2012   **Debit**   **Credit**

_____   _____

           _____   _____

           _____

Requirement 3

April 1, 2013   **Debit**   **Credit**

_____   _____

           _____   _____

           _____   _____

           _____

Name _____ Date _____ Course _____ Section _____

Exercise 5-18

		Wal-Mart	Target	Costco
Receivables turnover ratio	=	_____ _____	_____	_____
	=	[____]	[____]	[____]
Average collection period	=	_____ _____	_____	_____
	=	[____]	[____]	[____]

Exercise 5-19

Requirement 1

<u>December 31, 2012</u>   Debit   Credit

_____ _____ _____

_____ _____ _____

Requirement 2

<u>December 31, 2012</u>   Debit   Credit

_____ _____ _____

_____ _____ _____

_____

Requirement 3

	Percentage of receivables method	Percentage of credit sales method
Total Assets	_____	_____
Net Income	_____	_____

_____
_____
_____
_____
_____

   The McGraw-Hill Companies   *Financial Accounting*

Name _____ Date _____ Course _____ Section _____

Exercise 5-20

Requirement 1

December 31, 2012   Debit   Credit

_____ _____   _____

                  _____   _____

                  _____   _____

Requirement 2

December 31, 2012   Debit   Credit

_____   _____

                  _____   _____

                  _____   _____

Requirement 3

	Percentage of receivables method	Percentage of credit sales method
Total Assets	_____	_____
Net Income	_____	_____

_____
_____
_____
_____

Name _____ Date _____ Course _____ Section _____

Problem 5-1A

Revenue recognized in 2012

Scenario 1: _____

Scenario 2: _____

Scenario 3: _____

Scenario 4: _____

Problem 5-2A

Requirement 1

May 2   Debit   Credit

_____   _____

_____   _____

_____

May 7

_____   _____

_____   _____

_____

May 9

_____   _____

_____   _____

May 15

_____   _____

_____   _____

_____

Problem 5-2A Continued

May 20	Debit	Credit
_____	_____	
_____	_____	
	_____	_____

Requirement 2

Net sales	

Requirement 3

Outdoor Expo Partial Income Statement		
Net Tour Revenues		

Problem 5-3A

Requirement 1

June 12, 2012	Debit	Credit
_____	_____	
	_____	_____
	_____	_____

September 17, 2012		
_____	_____	
	_____	_____

Name _____ **Date** _____ **Course** _____ **Section** _____

Problem 5-3A Continued

December 31, 2012   **Debit**   **Credit**

_____   _____

    _____   _____

    _____

March 4, 2013

_____   _____

    _____   _____

    _____

May 20, 2013

_____

    _____   _____

    _____

July 2, 2013

_____

    _____   _____

    _____

October 19, 2013

_____   _____

    _____   _____

    _____

      The McGraw-Hill Companies   *Financial Accounting*

Name _____ Date _____ Course _____ Section _____

Problem 5-3A Continued

<u>December 31, 2013</u>   __Debit__   __Credit__

_____   _____   _____

                _____   _____

                _____

Requirement 2

Cash		Accounts Receivable

Dec. 31, 2012

Dec. 31, 2013

Dec. 31, 2012

Dec. 31, 2013

Allow. for Uncol. Accts.

Dec. 31, 2012

Dec. 31, 2013

Requirement 3

	2012	2013
Net realizable value		

Name _____ Date _____ Course _____ Section _____

Problem 5-4A

Requirement 1

Age Group	Amount Receivable	Estimated Percent Uncollectible	Estimated Amount Uncoll-ectible
Not yet due			_____
0-90 days past due			_____
91-180 days past due			_____
More than 180 days past due	_____		_____
Total	==========		==========

Requirement 2

December 31, 2012	Debit	Credit
_____	_____	_____
_____	_____	_____
_____		

Requirement 3

July 19, 2013	Debit	Credit
_____	_____	_____
_____	_____	_____
_____		

Requirement 4

September 30, 2013	Debit	Credit
_____	_____	_____
_____	_____	_____
_____		

September 30, 2013

_____	_____	_____
_____	_____	_____
_____		

Problem 5-5A

Requirement 1

_____
_____
_____
_____
_____
_____

Requirement 2

_____
_____

Requirement 3

_____
_____
_____
_____

Problem 5-6A

Requirement 1

	Debit	Credit
_____	_____	_____
_____		_____
_____		

Requirement 2

_____
_____
_____
_____

Requirement 3

	Debit	Credit
_____	_____	_____
_____		_____
_____		

Name _____ Date _____ Course _____ Section _____

Problem 5-6A Continued

_____

_____

_____

_____

_____

Requirement 4

_____

_____

_____

_____

Problem 5-7A

Requirement 1

<u>December 31, 2012</u>   Debit _____   Credit _____

_____   _____

_____   _____

_____

Requirement 2

_____

_____

_____

_____

_____

Requirement 3

_____

_____

_____

_____

_____

_____

Name _____ **Date** _____ **Course** _____ **Section** _____

Problem 5-8A

Requirement 1

<u>December 1, 2012</u>   **Debit**   **Credit**

_____   _____

     _____   _____

     _____

Requirement 2

<u>December 31, 2012</u>   **Debit**   **Credit**

_____   _____

     _____   _____

     _____

<u>December 31, 2013</u>

_____   _____

     _____   _____

     _____

<u>December 31, 2014</u>

_____   _____

     _____   _____

     _____

Name _____ Date _____ Course _____ Section _____

Problem 5-8A Continued

Requirement 3

<u>December 1, 2015</u>   **Debit**   **Credit**

_____

Name _____ Date _____ Course _____ Section _____

Problem 5-1B

Revenue recognized in 2012
Scenario 1: _____
Scenario 2: _____
Scenario 3: _____
Scenario 4: _____

Problem 5-2B

Requirement 1

<u>June 10</u>   <u>Debit</u>   <u>Credit</u>

_____   _____   _____

                    _____   _____   _____

<u>June 12</u>   _____

_____   _____   _____

                    _____   _____   _____

<u>June 13</u>   _____

_____   _____   _____

                    _____   _____   _____

<u>June 16</u>   _____

_____   _____   _____

                    _____   _____   _____

<u>June 19</u>   _____

_____   _____   _____

                    _____   _____   _____

                    _____

Name _____ Date _____ Course _____ Section _____

Problem 5-2B Continued

<u>June 20</u>   Debit   Credit

_____   _____

_____   _____

      _____   _____

      _____

<u>June 30</u>

_____   _____

_____   _____

      _____   _____

      _____

Requirement 2

Net sales	

Requirement 3

Data Recovery Services Partial Income Statement		
Net Sales		

Requirement 4

<u>June 25</u>

_____   _____

_____   _____

      _____   _____

      _____

Name _____ Date _____ Course _____ Section _____

Problem 5-2B Continued

Net Sales	

Problem 5-3B

Requirement 1

<u>February 2, 2012</u>   **Debit**   **Credit**

_____   _____

          _____   _____

          _____

<u>July 23, 2012</u>

_____   _____

          _____   _____

          _____

<u>December 31, 2012</u>

_____   _____

          _____   _____

          _____

<u>April 12, 2013</u>

_____   _____

          _____   _____

          _____

The McGraw-Hill Companies   *Financial Accounting*

Name _____ Date _____ Course _____ Section _____

Problem 5-3B Continued

June 28, 2013

	Debit	Credit
_____	_____	_____
_____	_____	_____
_____		

September 13, 2012

_____	_____	
_____	_____	_____
_____		

October 5, 2013

	Debit	Credit
_____	_____	_____
_____	_____	

December 31, 2013

_____	_____	
_____	_____	_____
_____	_____	_____

Requirement 2

Cash		Accounts Receivable	
Dec. 31, 2012		Dec. 31, 2012	
Dec. 31, 2013		Dec. 31, 2013	

Name _____ Date _____ Course _____ Section _____

Problem 5-3B Continued

Allow. for Uncol. Accts.

Dec. 31, 2012

Dec. 31, 2013

Requirement 3

	2012	2013
Net realizable value		

Problem 5-4B

Requirement 1

Age Group	Amount Receivable	Estimated Percent Uncollectible	Estimated Amount Uncollectible
Not yet due			
0-90 days past due			
91-180 days past due			
More than 180 days past due			
Total			

Requirement 2

December 31, 2012   Debit   Credit

_____ _____ _____

_____ _____

Requirement 3

April 3, 2013   Debit   Credit

_____ _____ _____

_____ _____

The McGraw-Hill Companies *Financial Accounting*

Name _____ Date _____ Course _____ Section _____

Problem 5-4B Continued

Requirement 4

__July 17, 2013__   __Debit__   __Credit__

_____   _____

      _____   _____

      _____

__July 17, 2013__

_____   _____

      _____   _____

      _____

Problem 5-5B

Requirement 1

_____
_____
_____
_____
_____
_____
_____

Requirement 2

_____
_____

Requirement 3

_____
_____
_____
_____

Name _____ **Date** _____ **Course** _____ **Section** _____

Problem 5-6B

Requirement 1

	Debit	Credit
_____	_____	_____
_____	_____	_____
_____		

Requirement 2

_____
_____
_____
_____
_____
_____

Requirement 3

_____
_____
_____
_____
_____
_____
_____
_____

Requirement 4

_____
_____
_____
_____
_____

Problem 5-7B

Requirement 1

	Debit	Credit
_____	_____	_____
_____	_____	_____

Name _____ Date _____ Course _____ Section _____

Problem 5-7B Continued

Requirement 2

_____
_____
_____
_____
_____
_____

Requirement 3

_____
_____
_____
_____
_____
_____

Problem 5-8B

Requirement 1

<u>April 1, 2012</u>   Debit   Credit

_____   _____

              _____   _____

              _____

Requirement 2

<u>December 31, 2012</u>   Debit   Credit

_____   _____

              _____   _____

              _____

<u>December 31, 2013</u>

_____   _____

              _____   _____

              _____

Name _____ Date _____ Course _____ Section _____

Problem 5-8B Continued

<u>December 31, 2014</u>   **Debit**   **Credit**

_____   _____

       _____   _____

       _____

Requirement 3

<u>April 1, 2015</u>   **Debit**   **Credit**

_____   _____

       _____   _____
       _____   _____
       _____   _____
       _____   _____
       _____   _____

       _____

Name _____ Date _____ Course _____ Section _____

Exercise 6-1

Cost of goods sold	

Exercise 6-2

Requirement 1

(a)	Date	Transaction	Number of units	Unit cost	Ending Inventory

(b)	Date	Transaction	Number of units	Unit cost	Cost of Goods Sold

(c) _____

(d) _____

_____

Requirement 2

(a)	Date	Transaction	Number of units	Unit cost	Ending Inventory

(b)	Date	Transaction	Number of units	Unit cost	Cost of Goods Sold

(c) _____

(d) _____

_____

Name _____ Date _____ Course _____ Section _____

Exercise 6-2 Continued

Requirement 3

Date	Transaction	Number of units	Unit cost	Total cost

(a) _____

(b) _____

(c) _____

(d) _____

_____

Requirement 4

Gross Profit	FIFO	LIFO	Weighted-average

_____

_____

_____

Exercise 6-3

Requirement 1

(a)	Date	Transaction	Number of units	Unit cost	Ending Inventory

(b)	Date	Transaction	Number of units	Unit cost	Cost of Goods Sold

Name _____ Date _____ Course _____ Section _____

Exercise 6-3 Continued

(c) _____

(d) _____
_____

Requirement 2

	Date	Transaction	Number of units	Unit cost	Ending Inventory
(a)					

	Date	Transaction	Number of units	Unit cost	Cost of Goods Sold
(b)					

(c) _____

(d) _____
_____

Requirement 3

Date	Transaction	Number of units	Unit cost	Total

(a) _____

(b) _____

(c) _____

(d) _____
_____

Name _____ Date _____ Course _____ Section _____

Exercise 6-3 Continued

Requirement 4

	FIFO	LIFO	Weighted-average
Gross Profit			

_____

_____

_____

Exercise 6-4

		Debit	Credit
_____		_____	
	_____		_____
	_____		_____
_____		_____	
	_____		_____
	_____		_____
_____		_____	
	_____		_____

Exercise 6-5

June 5		Debit	Credit
_____		_____	
	_____		_____
	_____		_____

Name _____ Date _____ Course _____ Section _____

Exercise 6-5 Continued

June 9   **Debit**   **Credit**

_____   _____

                    _____   _____

                            _____

June 16

_____   _____

                    _____   _____

                            _____

                    _____   _____

                            _____

Exercise 6-6

Requirement 1

June 5   **Debit**   **Credit**

_____   _____

                    _____   _____

                            _____

June 12

_____   _____

                    _____   _____

                            _____

Name _____ Date _____ Course _____ Section _____

Exercise 6-6 Continued

Requirement 2

<u>June 12</u>   Debit   Credit

_____   _____   _____

        _____   _____

        _____   _____

Exercise 6-7

Requirement 1

<u>May 2</u>   Debit   Credit

_____   _____   _____

        _____   _____

        _____

<u>May 3</u>

_____   _____

        _____   _____

        _____

<u>May 5</u>

_____   _____

        _____   _____

        _____

Name _____ Date _____ Course _____ Section _____

Exercise 6-7 Continued

May 10   Debit   Credit

_____   _____   _____

                _____   _____

                _____

May 30

_____

                _____   _____

                _____

_____   _____   _____

                _____   _____

                _____

Requirement 2

May 24   Debit   Credit

_____   _____   _____

                _____   _____

                _____

Exercise 6-8

July 5   Debit   Credit

_____   _____   _____

                _____   _____

                _____

Name _____ **Date** _____ **Course** _____ **Section** _____

Exercise 6-8 Continued

<u>July 8</u>   **Debit**   **Credit**

_____   _____   _____

             _____   _____

             _____

<u>July 13</u>

_____   _____

             _____   _____

             _____   _____

             _____

<u>July 28</u>

_____   _____

             _____   _____

             _____   _____

_____   _____

             _____   _____

             _____

Exercise 6-9

<u>August 6</u>   **Debit**   **Credit**

_____   _____

             _____   _____

             _____

Name _____ **Date** _____ **Course** _____ **Section** _____

Exercise 6-9 Continued

August 7   __**Debit**__   __**Credit**__

_____   _____   _____

                    _____   _____

                    _____

August 10

_____   _____

                    _____

                    _____

August 14

_____   _____

                    _____   _____

                    _____   _____

                    _____

August 23

_____   _____

                    _____   _____

                    _____

_____   _____

                    _____   _____

                    _____

Name _____ **Date** _____ **Course** _____ **Section** _____

Exercise 6-10

August 6

	Debit	Credit

_____ _____

_____ _____

_____

_____ _____

_____ _____

_____ _____

August 10

_____ _____

_____ _____

_____

August 14

_____ _____

_____ _____

_____ _____

_____

Name _____ Date _____ Course _____ Section _____

Exercise 6-11

Wayman Corporation Multiple-step Income Statement For the year ended December 31, 2012		
Net sales		
Operating income		
Net income		

Exercise 6-12

Requirement 1

Tisdale Incorporated Multiple-step Income Statement For the year ended December 31, 2012		
Net sales		
Operating income		
Net income		

Requirement 2

_____

_____

_____

_____

_____

_____

Name _____ Date _____ Course _____ Section _____

Exercise 6-13

Requirement 1

Inventory	Quantity	Lower of Cost or Market	Ending Inventory
Furniture			_____
Electronics			_____
			_____

Requirement 2

	Debit	Credit
_____	_____	_____
_____		_____
_____		

Requirement 3

_____

_____

_____

_____

_____

Exercise 6-14

Requirement 1

Inventory	Quantity	Lower of Cost or Market	Ending Inventory
Shirts			_____
MegaDriver			_____
MegaDriver II			_____
			_____

Requirement 2

	Debit	Credit
_____	_____	_____
_____	_____	_____
_____		

Name _____ **Date** _____ **Course** _____ **Section** _____

Exercise 6-14 Continued

Requirement 3

_____
_____
_____
_____

Exercise 6-15

Requirement 1

	Lewis	Clark
Beginning inventory		
Cost of goods sold		

Requirement 2

				Lewis		Clark
Inventory turnover ratio	=		=		=	
			=		=	

Requirement 3

				Lewis		Clark
Average days in inventory	=		=		=	
			=		=	

Requirement 4

_____
_____
_____
_____
_____

Name _____ Date _____ Course _____ Section _____

Exercise 6-16

Requirement 1

		Gross profit	Operating Income	Income before income taxes	Net Income
Henry					
Grace					
James					

Requirement 2

				Henry	Grace	James
Gross profit ratio	=					
	=					

_____

_____

Exercise 6-17

Requirement 1

May 2   Debit   Credit

_____   _____

_____   _____

May 3

_____   _____

_____   _____

May 5

_____   _____

_____   _____

Name _____ Date _____ Course _____ Section _____

Exercise 6-17 Continued

May 10   **Debit**   **Credit**

_____   _____

            _____   _____
            _____   _____

            _____

May 30

_____   _____   _____

            _____   _____

            _____

Requirement 2

May 31   **Debit**   **Credit**

_____   _____
_____   _____
_____   _____
_____   _____

            _____   _____
            _____   _____

            _____   _____

Exercise 6-18

Requirement 1

July 5   **Debit**   **Credit**

_____   _____

            _____   _____

            _____

Name _____ Date _____ Course _____ Section _____

Exercise 6-18 Continued

<u>July 8</u>   **Debit**   **Credit**

_____   _____

                _____   _____

                _____

<u>July 13</u>

_____   _____

                _____   _____
                _____   _____

                _____

<u>July 28</u>

_____   _____

                _____   _____

                _____

Requirement 2

<u>July 31</u>   **Debit**   **Credit**

_____   _____
_____   _____
_____   _____
_____   _____

                _____   _____
                _____   _____

                _____

Name _____ Date _____ Course _____ Section _____

Exercise 6-19

Requirement 1

<u>August 6</u>   Debit   Credit

_____   _____

                    _____   _____

                    _____

<u>August 7</u>

_____   _____

                    _____   _____

                    _____

<u>August 10</u>

_____   _____

                    _____   _____

                    _____

<u>August 14</u>

_____   _____

                    _____   _____

                    _____

<u>August 23</u>

_____   _____

                    _____   _____

                    _____

The McGraw-Hill Companies   *Financial Accounting*

Exercise 6-19 Continued

Requirement 2

August 31	Debit	Credit
_____	_____	
_____	_____	
_____	_____	
_____	_____	
_____		_____
_____		_____
_____		_____
_____		

Exercise 6-20

Requirement 1

_____
_____
_____
_____
_____
_____
_____

Requirement 2

	Balance Sheet			Income Statement		
Year	Assets	Liabilities	Stockholders' equity	Revenues	Cost of goods sold	Gross Profit
Current	_____	_____	_____	_____	_____	_____
Following	_____	_____	_____	_____	_____	_____

Name _____ Date _____ Course _____ Section _____

Problem 6-1A

Requirement 1

Date	Transaction	Number of units	Unit cost	Ending Inventory

Date	Transaction	Number of units	Unit cost	Cost of Goods Sold

Requirement 2

Date	Transaction	Number of units	Unit cost	Ending Inventory

Date	Transaction	Number of units	Unit cost	Cost of Goods Sold

Requirement 3

Date	Transaction	Number of units	Unit cost	Ending Inventory

Date	Transaction	Number of units	Unit cost	Cost of Goods Sold

Problem 6-1A Continued

Requirement 4

Date	Transaction	Number of units	Unit cost	Cost of Goods Sold

_____

_____

_____

Problem 6-2A

Requirement 1

Date	Transaction	Number of units	Unit cost	Ending Inventory

Date	Transaction	Number of units	Unit cost	Cost of Goods Sold

Requirement 2

Date	Transaction	Number of units	Unit cost	Ending Inventory

Date	Transaction	Number of units	Unit cost	Cost of Goods Sold

Name _____ **Date** _____ **Course** _____ **Section** _____

Problem 6-2A Continued

Requirement 3

Date	Transaction	Number of units	Unit cost	Ending Inventory

Date	Transaction	Number of units	Unit cost	Cost of Goods Sold

Requirement 4

Date	Transaction	Number of units	Unit cost	Total Cost

Ending Inventory		
Cost of Goods Sold		

Requirement 5

	Specific Identification	FIFO	LIFO	Weighted average Cost
Gross profit				

Requirement 6

_____

_____

_____

_____

_____

_____

Name _____ Date _____ Course _____ Section _____

Problem 6-2A Continued

Requirement 7

<u>March 31</u>   **Debit**   **Credit**

_____   _____

     _____   _____

Problem 6-3A

Requirement 1

<u>July 3</u>   **Debit**   **Credit**

_____

     _____   _____

     _____   _____

<u>July 4</u>

_____

     _____   _____

     _____

<u>July 9</u>

_____   _____

     _____   _____

     _____

Problem 6-3A Continued

		Debit	**Credit**

<u>July 11</u>

_____   _____   _____

                           _____   _____
                           _____   _____
                           _____

<u>July 12</u>

_____   _____

                           _____   _____
                           _____

_____   _____

                           _____   _____

                           _____

<u>July 15</u>

_____   _____

                           _____   _____
                           _____

<u>July 18</u>

_____

                           _____   _____
                           _____

Name _____ Date _____ Course _____ Section _____

Problem 6-3A Continued

<u>July 22</u>   Debit   Credit

_____   _____

                  _____   _____

                  _____

_____   _____

                  _____   _____

                  _____

<u>July 28</u>

_____   _____

                  _____   _____

                  _____

<u>July 30</u>   _____

_____   _____

                  _____   _____

                  _____

Requirement 2

CD City Multiple-step Income Statement (partial) For the month of July		
Gross Profit		

 Financial Accounting

Name _____ Date _____ Course _____ Section _____

Problem 6-4A

Requirement 1

Inventory items	Quantity	Cost Per unit	Total Cost
Vans			
Trucks			
2-door Sedans			
4-door Sedans			
Sports Cars			
SUVs			

Requirement 2

Inventory items	Quantity	Cost Per unit	Market (replacement cost) per unit	Lower of cost or market	Total
Vans					
Trucks					
2-door Sedans					
4-door Sedans					
Sports Cars					
SUVs					
Total					

Requirement 3

_____

_____

_____

	Debit	Credit

Requirement 4

_____

_____

_____

The McGraw-Hill Companies   *Financial Accounting*

Name _____ Date _____ Course _____ Section _____

Problem 6-5A

Requirement 1

Date	Transaction	Number of units	Unit cost	Ending Inventory

Date	Transaction	Number of units	Unit cost	Cost of Goods Sold

Requirement 2

Date	Transaction	Number of units	Unit cost	Ending Inventory

Date	Transaction	Number of units	Unit cost	Cost of Goods Sold

Requirement 3

	Ending Inventory		
	Cost	Market	Lower of cost or market
FIFO			
LIFO			

Name _____ Date _____ Course _____ Section _____

Problem 6-5A Continued

(a) FIFO   ___Debit___   ___Credit___

_____   _____

                    _____   _____

                    _____   _____

(b) LIFO

_____   _____

                    _____   _____

                    _____   _____

Problem 6-6A

Requirement 1

October 4   ___Debit___   ___Credit___

_____   _____

                    _____   _____

                    _____   _____

October 5

_____   _____

                    _____   _____

                    _____   _____

October 9

_____   _____

                    _____   _____

                    _____   _____

Name _____ Date _____ Course _____ Section _____

Problem 6-6A Continued

October 12		Debit	Credit
_____		_____	
	_____		_____
	_____		_____
	_____		

October 15

_____		_____	
	_____		_____
	_____		
_____		_____	
	_____		_____
	_____		

October 19

_____		_____	
	_____		_____
	_____		

October 20

_____		_____	
	_____		_____
	_____		

Name _____ Date _____ Course _____ Section _____

Problem 6-6A Continued

October 22   **Debit**   **Credit**

_____

      _____

      _____

_____

      _____

      _____

Requirement 2

October 31   **Debit**   **Credit**

_____

      _____

      _____

Requirement 3

October 31   **Debit**   **Credit**

_____

      _____

      _____

Requirement 4

Bowser Co. Multiple-step Income Statement (partial) For the month of October	
Gross Profit	

Problem 6-7A

Requirement 1

Baskin-Robbins Multiple-step Income Statement For the month of July, 2012		
Net sales:		
Net sales		
Cost of goods sold		
Gross Profit		
Operating income		
Income before income taxes		
Net income		

Requirement 2

Inventory turnover ratio = ⬚ = ⬚ = ⬚

_____
_____
_____
_____

Requirement 3

Gross profit ratio = ⬚ = ⬚ = ⬚

Name _____ **Date** _____ **Course** _____ **Section** _____

Problem 6-8A

Requirement 1

		Company 1	Company 2

Inventory turnover ratio $=$ [   ] $=$ [   ] [   ]

$=$ [   ] [   ]

Requirement 2

		Company 1	Company 2

Gross profit ratio $=$ [   ] $=$ [   ] [   ]

$=$ [   ] [   ]

Requirement 3

_____
_____
_____
_____
_____
_____
_____
_____
_____

Problem 6-9A

Requirement 1

July 3   Debit   Credit

_____   _____
                    _____   _____
                    _____   _____

The McGraw-Hill Companies *Financial Accounting*

Name _____ Date _____ Course _____ Section _____

Problem 6-9A Continued

July 4		Debit	Credit
_____		_____	
	_____		_____
	_____		

July 9			
_____		_____	
	_____		_____
	_____		

July 11			
_____		_____	
	_____		_____
	_____		_____
	_____		

July 12			
_____		_____	
	_____		_____
	_____		

July 15			
_____		_____	
	_____		_____
	_____		

Name _____ Date _____ Course _____ Section _____

Problem 6-9A Continued

<u>July 18</u>   Debit   Credit

_____

                    _____   _____

                    _____

<u>July 22</u>

_____   _____   _____

                    _____   _____

                    _____

<u>July 28</u>

_____   _____   _____

                    _____   _____

                    _____

<u>July 30</u>

_____   _____   _____

                    _____   _____

                    _____

Requirement 2

<u>July 31</u>   Debit   Credit

_____   _____
_____   _____
_____   _____
_____   _____

                    _____   _____
                    _____   _____
                    _____   _____

                    _____

Name _____ Date _____ Course _____ Section _____

Problem 6-9A Continued

Requirement 3

CD City Multiple-step Income Statement (partial) For the month of July		
Net sales		
Gross Profit		

Name _____ Date _____ Course _____ Section _____

Problem 6-10A

Requirement 1

		2009	2010	2011	2012
Gross profit ratio	=	⬜	⬜	⬜	⬜
	=	⬜	⬜	⬜	⬜

Requirement 2

		2009	2010	2011	2012
Gross profit ratio	=	⬜	⬜	⬜	⬜
	=	⬜	⬜	⬜	⬜

_____
_____
_____
_____
_____
_____
_____
_____
_____

Requirement 3

_____
_____
_____
_____
_____
_____
_____
_____
_____
_____
_____

The McGraw-Hill Companies   *Financial Accounting*

Name _____ Date _____ Course _____ Section _____

Problem 6-1B

Requirement 1

Date	Transaction	Number of units	Unit cost	Ending Inventory

Date	Transaction	Number of units	Unit cost	Cost of Goods Sold

Requirement 2

Date	Transaction	Number of units	Unit cost	Ending Inventory

Date	Transaction	Number of units	Unit cost	Cost of Goods Sold

Requirement 3

Date	Transaction	Number of units	Unit cost	Ending Inventory

Name _____ Date _____ Course _____ Section _____

Problem 6-1B Continued

Date	Transaction	Number of units	Unit cost	Ending Inventory

Requirement 4

Date	Transaction	Number of units	Unit cost	Cost of Goods Sold

_____

_____

_____

Problem 6-2B

Requirement 1

Date	Transaction	Number of units	Unit cost	Ending Inventory

Date	Transaction	Number of units	Unit cost	Cost of Goods Sold

Name _____ Date _____ Course _____ Section _____

Problem 6-2B Continued

Requirement 2

Date	Transaction	Number of units	Unit cost	Ending Inventory

Date	Transaction	Number of units	Unit cost	Cost of Goods Sold

Requirement 3

Date	Transaction	Number of units	Unit cost	Ending Inventory

Date	Transaction	Number of units	Unit cost	Cost of Goods Sold

Requirement 4

Date	Transaction	Number of units	Unit cost	Ending Inventory

_____

_____

_____

 Financial Accounting

Name _____ Date _____ Course _____ Section _____

Problem 6-2B Continued

Requirement 5

	Specific Identification	FIFO	LIFO	Weighted average Cost
Gross profit				

Requirement 6

_____

_____

_____

_____

_____

_____

Requirement 7

August 31   Debit   Credit

_____   _____

_____   _____

_____

Problem 6-3B

Requirement 1

June 2   Debit   Credit

_____   _____

_____   _____

_____

June 4

_____   _____

_____   _____

_____

Name _____ Date _____ Course _____ Section _____

Problem 6-3B Continued

<u>June 8</u>   Debit   Credit

_____   _____   _____
                    _____   _____

<u>June 10</u>

_____   _____   _____
_____   _____   _____
_____   _____   _____
_____

<u>June 11</u>

_____   _____   _____
_____   _____   _____
_____   _____   _____
_____   _____   _____

<u>June 18</u>

_____   _____   _____
_____   _____   _____
_____

<u>June 20</u>

_____   _____   _____
_____   _____   _____
_____

Name _____ Date _____ Course _____ Section _____

Problem 6-3B Continued

<u>June 23</u>   Debit   Credit

_____

      _____   _____

      _____   _____

_____   _____

      _____   _____

      _____

<u>June 26</u>

_____   _____

      _____   _____

<u>June 28</u>   _____

_____   _____

      _____   _____

      _____

Requirement 2

| Circuit Country | | |
| Multiple-step Income Statement (partial) | | |
For the month of June		
Gross Profit		

The McGraw-Hill Companies   *Financial Accounting*

Name _____ **Date** _____ **Course** _____ **Section** _____

Problem 6-4B

Requirement 1

Inventory items	Quantity	Cost Per unit	Total Cost
Hammers			
Saws			
Screwdrivers			
Drills			
1-gallon paint cans			
Paint brushes			

Requirement 2

Inventory items	Quantity	Cost Per unit	Market (replacement cost) per unit	Lower of cost or market	Total
Hammers					
Saws					
Screwdrivers					
Drills					
1-gallon paint cans					
Paint brushes					
Total					

Requirement 3

_____

_____

_____

	Debit	Credit
_____	_____	_____
_____	_____	_____
_____	_____	_____

Requirement 4

_____

_____

_____

Name _____ Date _____ Course _____ Section _____

Problem 6-5B

Requirement 1

Date	Transaction	Number of units	Unit cost	Ending Inventory

Date	Transaction	Number of units	Unit cost	Cost of Goods Sold

Requirement 2

Date	Transaction	Number of units	Unit cost	Ending Inventory

Date	Transaction	Number of units	Unit cost	Cost of Goods Sold

Requirement 3

	Ending Inventory		Lower of cost or market
	Cost	Market	
FIFO			
LIFO			

Problem 6-5B Continued

(a) FIFO   **Debit**   **Credit**

_____   _____

                _____   _____

(b) LIFO

_____   _____

                _____   _____

                _____

Problem 6-6B

Requirement 1

November 2   **Debit**   **Credit**

_____   _____

                _____   _____

                _____

November 3

_____   _____

                _____   _____

                _____

November 9

_____   _____

                _____   _____

                _____

Name _____ Date _____ Course _____ Section _____

Problem 6-6B Continued

<u>November 11</u>   __Debit__   __Credit__

_____   _____

      _____   _____

      _____   _____

      _____

<u>November 16</u>

_____   _____

      _____   _____

_____   _____

      _____

      _____

<u>November 20</u>

_____   _____

      _____   _____

      _____

<u>November 21</u>

_____   _____

      _____   _____

      _____

           The McGraw-Hill Companies   _Financial Accounting_

Name _____ Date _____ Course _____ Section _____

Problem 6-6B Continued

<u>November 24</u>   **Debit**   **Credit**

_____   _____

         _____   _____

         _____   _____

_____   _____

         _____   _____

         _____

Requirement 2

<u>November 30</u>   **Debit**   **Credit**

_____   _____

         _____   _____

         _____

Requirement 3

<u>November 30</u>   **Debit**   **Credit**

____ _____   _____

         _____   _____

         _____

Requirement 4

Yoshi Inc. Multiple-step Income Statement (partial) For the month of November	
Gross Profit	

     The McGraw-Hill Companies   *Financial Accounting*

Name _____ Date _____ Course _____ Section _____

Problem 6-7B

Requirement 1

Toys "R" Us Multiple-step Income Statement For the month of March, 2012		
Net sales:		
Gross Profit		
Operating income		
Income before income taxes		
Net income		

Requirement 2

Inventory turnover ratio = [   ] = [   ] = [   ]

_____

_____

_____

_____

Requirement 3

Gross profit ratio = [   ] = [   ] = [   ]

Name _____ Date _____ Course _____ Section _____

Problem 6-8B

Requirement 1

		Company 1	Company 2
Inventory turnover ratio	=		
	=		

Requirement 2

		Company 1	Company 2
Gross profit ratio	=		
	=		

Requirement 3

_____

_____

_____

_____

_____

_____

_____

_____

_____

Problem 6-9B

Requirement 1

June 2	Debit	Credit

Name _____ Date _____ Course _____ Section _____

Problem 6-9B Continued

June 4			Debit	Credit

_____   _____

                    _____   _____

                                   _____

June 8

_____   _____

                    _____   _____

                                   _____

June 10

_____   _____

                    _____   _____
                    _____   _____

                                   _____

June 11

_____   _____

                    _____   _____

                                   _____

June 18

_____   _____

                    _____   _____

                    _____

The McGraw-Hill Companies   *Financial Accounting*

Name _____ Date _____ Course _____ Section _____

Problem 6-9B Continued

June 20   Debit   Credit

_____   _____

                   _____   _____

                   _____

June 20

_____   _____

                   _____   _____

                   _____

June 26

_____   _____

                   _____   _____

                   _____

June 28

_____   _____

                   _____   _____

                   _____

Requirement 2

June 30   Debit   Credit

_____   _____
_____   _____
_____   _____
_____   _____

                   _____   _____
                   _____   _____
                   _____   _____

                   _____

Name _____ Date _____ Course _____ Section _____

Problem 6-9B Continued

Requirement 3

Circuit Country Multiple-step Income Statement (partial) For the month of June		
Net sales		
Gross Profit		

Name _____ Date _____ Course _____ Section _____

Problem 6-10B

Requirement 1

Date	Transaction	Number of units	Unit cost	Ending Inventory

Date	Transaction	Number of units	Unit cost	Cost of Goods Sold

Requirement 2

Date	Transaction	Number of units	Unit cost	Ending Inventory

Date	Transaction	Number of units	Unit cost	Ending Inventory

Requirement 3 & 4

	2012	2013
(a) ending inventory		
(b) retained earnings		
(c) cost of goods sold		
(d) net income		

Name _____ Date _____ Course _____ Section _____

Exercise 7-1

Calculating the cost of land

Total Cost of Land	

_____

_____

_____

_____

_____

_____

Exercise 7-2

	Debit	Credit
_____	_____	
_____	_____	
_____		_____
_____		_____
_____		

Calculation for Total Cost of Equipment :

Total cost	

Exercise 7-3

	Estimated Fair Value	Allocation Percentage	Amount of Basket	Recorded Amount
Land				
Building				
Equipment				
Total				

Name _____ Date _____ Course _____ Section _____

Exercise 7-4

	Debit	Credit
_____	_____	
_____	_____	
_____	_____	
_____		_____
_____		

Exercise 7-5

(1) _____

Calculation :

Total	

(2) _____

Calculation :

Total	

(3) _____

Calculation :

Total	

Name _____ Date _____ Course _____ Section _____

Exercise 7-6

		Accum Depreci	
Goodwill			

Exercise 7-7

Requirement 1

Patent costs capitalized :

Total costs capitalized	

Requirement 2

Expense items on income statement :

Total Research and Development Expense	

Requirement 3

_____

_____

_____

Exercise 7-8

	List A		List B
____	1.	Depreciation	a. Exclusive right to display a word, a symbol,
____	2.	Goodwill	or an emblem.
____	3.	Amortization	b. Exclusive right to benefit from a creative work.
____	4.	Natural resources	c. Assets that represent contractual rights.
____	5.	Intangible assets	d. Oil and gas deposits, timber tracts, and mineral
____	6.	Copyright	deposits.
____	7.	Trademark	e. Purchase price less fair market value of net
			identifiable assets.
			f. The allocation of cost for plant and equipment.
			g. The allocation of cost for intangible assets.

Exercise 7-9

Expenditure	Account Debited	Amount
1		
2		
3		
4		
5		
6		

Exercise 7-10

1.   **Straight-line**

Depreciation Expense	=		=	

2.   **Double-declining-balance**

Depreciation Expense	=		=	

3.   **Activity-based**

Depreciation Expense	=		=		=	

Exercise 7-11

Requirement 1

Straight-line				
Depreciation Expense	=		=	

Requirement 2

	Double-declining-balance					
	Calculation			**End of Year Amounts**		
Year	Beginning Book Value	x	Depreciation Rate	=	Depreciation Expense	Accumulated Depreciation	Book Value
1							
2							
3							
4							
Total							

Name _____ Date _____ Course _____ Section _____

Exercise 7-16 Continued

<u>December 31, 2014</u>

_____   _____
        _____   _____
        _____

Requirement 2

Balance in patent account

Patents

_____   _____
_____   _____
_____   _____
_____   _____

Exercise 7-17

Requirement 1

	Debit	Credit
_____	_____	
_____		
_____	_____	_____
_____		

Requirement 2

	Debit	Credit
_____	_____	
_____	_____	
_____	_____	
_____	_____	_____
_____		

Name _____ Date _____ Course _____ Section _____

Exercise 7-18

Requirement 1

Find the fair value of the new land	
Fair value of the new land	

Requirement 2

	Debit	Credit
_____	_____	_____
	_____	_____
	_____	_____
	_____	_____
	_____	

Exercise 7-19

Return on Assets = [_____] = [_____] = [_____]

Profit Margin = [_____] = [_____] = [_____]

Asset Turnover = [_____] = [_____] = [_____]

Exercise 7-20

Requirement 1

_____

_____

_____

_____

_____

_____

_____

_____

Name _____ Date _____ Course _____ Section _____

Exercise 7-20 Continued

Requirement 2

_____
_____
_____
_____
_____
_____
_____
_____
_____

Name _____ Date _____ Course _____ Section _____

Problem 7-1A

	Land	Building
Totals		

_____
_____

Problem 7-2A

Requirement 1

Total Equipment	

_____
_____

Requirement 2

_____
_____
_____
_____
_____

Problem 7-3A

Requirement 1

Goodwill		

 Financial Accounting

Name _____ Date _____ Course _____ Section _____

Problem 7-3A Continued

Requirement 2

	Debit	Credit
_____	_____	_____
_____		
_____		
_____	_____	
_____		_____
_____		
_____		

Problem 7-4A

(1) _____
(2) _____
(3) _____
(4) _____
(5) _____
(6) _____

_____
_____
_____
_____
_____

Problem 7-5A

Requirement 1

University Car Wash						
	Calculation		=	End of Year Amounts		
Year	Allocation Base	x	Depreciation Rate	Depreciation Expense	Accumulated Depreciation	Book Value
1						
2						
3						
4						
5						
6						
Total						

 Financial Accounting

Name _____ Date _____ Course _____ Section _____

Problem 7-5A Continued

Requirement 2

	University Car Wash					
	Calculation				**End of Year Amounts**	
Year	**Beginning Book Value**	**x**	**Depreciation Rate**	**=**	**Depreciation Expense**	**Accumulated Depreciation**	**Book Value**
1							
2							
3							
4							
5							
6							
Total							

Requirement 3

	University Car Wash					
	Calculation				**End of Year Amounts**	
Year	**Hours Used**	**x**	**Depreciation Rate**	**=**	**Depreciation Expense**	**Accumulated Depreciation**	**Book Value**
1							
2							
3							
4							
5							
6							
Total							

Problem 7-6A

Requirement 1

	Debit	Credit
a. _____	_____	_____
_____		
_____		
b. _____	_____	_____
_____		_____
_____		

Name _____ Date _____ Course _____ Section _____

Problem 7-6A Continued

	Debit	Credit
c. _____	_____	_____
_____		
_____		

Requirement 2

University Testing Services Balance Sheet December 31, 2012 (Intangible Assets Section)	
Intangible Assets	
Total Intangible Assets	

Problem 7-7A

Requirement 1

	Debit	Credit
_____	_____	_____
_____		_____
_____		
_____	_____	
_____		

Requirement 2

	Debit	Credit
_____	_____	_____
_____	_____	_____
_____		

Name _____ Date _____ Course _____ Section _____

Problem 7-7A Continued

Requirement 3

Solich Sandwich Shop			
December 31, 2012			
	Cost	Accumulated Depreciation	Book Value
Land			
Building			
Equipment			
Patent			

Problem 7-8A

Requirement 1

_____
_____
_____
_____

Requirement 2

Book value at the end of year 2	

Requirement 3

Requirement 4

	Debit	Credit

Name _____ Date _____ Course _____ Section _____

Problem 7-9A

Requirement 1

<u>Dell</u>

Return on Assets	=		=		=
Profit Margin	=		=		=
Asset Turnover	=		=		=

Requirement 2

<u>Apple</u>

Return on Assets	=		=		=
Profit Margin	=		=		=
Asset Turnover	=		=		=

Requirement 3

_____

_____

_____

_____

_____

Name _____ Date _____ Course _____ Section _____

Problem 7-10A

Requirement 1

Sandwiches Only

Return on Assets	=		=	

Profit Margin	=		=	

Asset Turnover	=		=	

Requirement 2

Sandwiches and Smoothies

Return on Assets	=		=	

Profit Margin	=		=	

Asset Turnover	=		=	

Requirement 3

_____

_____

_____

_____

_____

Name _____ Date _____ Course _____ Section _____

Problem 7-1B

	Land	Building
Totals		

Problem 7-2B

Requirement 1

Total Equipment	

Requirement 2

Problem 7-3B

Requirement 1

Goodwill		

Name _____ Date _____ Course _____ Section _____

Problem 7-3B Continued

Requirement 2

	Debit	Credit
_____	_____	_____
_____	_____	_____
_____	_____	_____
_____	_____	_____
_____	_____	
_____	_____	
_____		

Problem 7-4B

(1) _____
(2) _____
(3) _____
(4) _____
(5) _____
(6) _____

_____
_____
_____
_____
_____
_____

Problem 7-5B

Requirement 1

	Cheetah Copy					
	Calculation				**End of Year Amounts**	
Year	**Allocation Base**	**x**	**Depreciation Rate**	**=**	**Depreciation Expense**	**Accumulated Depreciation**	**Book Value**
1							
2							
3							
4							
Total							

Name _____ Date _____ Course _____ Section _____

Problem 7-5B Continued

Requirement 2

	Cheetah Copy					
	Calculation				End of Year Amounts	
Year	Beginning Book Value	x	Depreciation Rate	=	Depreciation Expense	Accumulated Depreciation	Book Value
1							
2							
3							
4							
Total							

Requirement 3

	Cheetah Copy					
	Calculation				End of Year Amounts	
Year	Hours Used	x	Depreciation Rate	=	Depreciation Expense	Accumulated Depreciation	Book Value
1							
2							
3							
4							
Total							

Problem 7-6B

Requirement 1

	Debit	Credit

a. _____   _____   _____

    _____   _____

    _____

b. _____   _____   _____

    _____   _____

    _____

Name _____ Date _____ Course _____ Section _____

Problem 7-6B Continued

	Debit	Credit
c. _____	_____	_____
_____	_____	
_____		

Requirement 2

Lettuce Express Balance Sheet December 31, 2012 (Intangible Assets Section)	
Intangible Assets	
Total Intangible Assets	

Problem 7-7B

Requirement 1

	Debit	Credit
_____	_____	_____
_____	_____	_____
_____		
_____	_____	_____
_____		
_____		

Requirement 2

	Debit	Credit
_____	_____	_____
_____	_____	_____
_____	_____	_____

Name _____ Date _____ Course _____ Section _____

Problem 7-7B Continued

Requirement 3

Togo's Sandwich Shop			
December 31, 2012			
	Cost	Accumulated Depreciation	Book Value
Land			
Building			
Equipment			
Patent			

Problem 7-8B

Requirement 1

_____
_____
_____
_____

Requirement 2

Book value at the end of year 3	

Requirement 3

Requirement 4

	Debit	Credit

Name _____ Date _____ Course _____ Section _____

Problem 7-9B

Requirement 1

<u>Nike</u>

Return on Assets = [   ] = [   ] = [   ]

Profit Margin = [   ] = [   ] = [   ]

Asset Turnover = [   ] = [   ] = [   ]

Requirement 2

<u>Under Armour</u>

Return on Assets = [   ] = [   ] = [   ]

Profit Margin = [   ] = [   ] = [   ]

Asset Turnover = [   ] = [   ] = [   ]

Requirement 3

_____

_____

_____

_____

Name _____ Date _____ Course _____ Section _____

Problem 7-10B

Requirement 1

<u>Cars Only</u>

| Return on Assets | = | | = | | = | |

| Profit Margin | = | | = | | = | |

| Asset Turnover | = | | = | | = | |

Requirement 2

<u>Cars and Boats</u>

| Return on Assets | = | | = | | = | |

| Profit Margin | = | | = | | = | |

| Asset Turnover | = | | = | | = | |

Requirement 3

_____
_____
_____
_____
_____

Exercise 8-1

Reporting Method :

C. Current Liability
L. Long-term liability
D. Disclosure note only
N. Not reported

Item

_____	1. Accounts payable.
_____	2. Current portion of long-term debt.
_____	3. Sales tax collected from customers.
_____	4. Notes payable due next year.
_____	5. Notes payable due in two years.
_____	6. Customer advances.
_____	7. Commercial paper.
_____	8. Unused line of credit.
_____	9. A contingent liability that is probable of occurring within the next and can be estimated.
_____	10. A contingent liability that is reasonably possible of occurring within next year and can be estimated.

Exercise 8-2

November 1, 2012   Debit   Credit

_____   _____

_____   _____

_____

December 31, 2012

_____   _____

_____   _____

_____

Name _____ Date _____ Course _____ Section _____

Exercise 8-2 Continued

January 31, 2013   **Debit**   **Credit**

_____   _____
_____   _____
_____   _____

          _____   _____

          _____

Exercise 8-3

August 1, 2012   **Debit**   **Credit**

_____   _____

          _____

          _____

December 31, 2012

_____   _____

          _____   _____

          _____

January 31, 2013

_____   _____
_____   _____
_____   _____

          _____   _____

          _____

Name _____ Date _____ Course _____ Section _____

Exercise 8-4

<u>August 1, 2012</u>   **Debit**   **Credit**

_____   _____

                _____   _____

                _____

<u>December 31, 2012</u>

_____   _____

                _____   _____

                _____

<u>January 31, 2013</u>

_____   _____

                _____   _____
                _____   _____
                _____   _____

                _____

Exercise 8-5

1. _____   x   _____   x   _____   =   _____

2. _____   x   _____   x   _____   =   _____

3. _____   x   _____   x   _____   =   _____

4. _____   x   _____   x   _____   =   _____

Name _____ Date _____ Course _____ Section _____

Exercise 8-6

<u>January 13</u>   Debit   Credit

_____   _____   _____

                 _____   _____

                 _____

<u>February 1</u>

_____   _____   _____

                 _____   _____

                 _____

<u>May 1</u>

_____   _____

_____   _____

                 _____   _____

                 _____

Exercise 8-7

Requirement 1

Actual Direct Deposit		

Requirement 2

Total Payroll Tax Expense	

Requirement 3

_____

_____

_____

The McGraw-Hill Companies   *Financial Accounting*

Name _____ Date _____ Course _____ Section _____

Exercise 8-8

Requirement 1

<u>January 31</u>   Debit   Credit
                                              _____   _____

_____   _____

                      _____   _____
                      _____   _____
                      _____   _____
                      _____   _____
                      _____   _____

                      _____

Requirement 2

<u>January 31</u>   Debit   Credit
                                              _____   _____

_____   _____

          _____   _____

          _____

Requirement 3

<u>January 31</u>   Debit   Credit
                                              _____   _____

_____   _____

          _____   _____
          _____   _____

          _____

Exercise 8-9

January 31   Debit   Credit

_____   _____

          _____   _____

          _____   _____

          _____   _____

          _____   _____

          _____

January 31

_____   _____

          _____   _____

          _____   _____

          _____

Exercise 8-10

Requirement 1

                                     Debit   Credit

_____   _____

          _____   _____

          _____

Requirement 2

                                     Debit   Credit

_____   _____

          _____   _____

          _____

Name _____ Date _____ Course _____ Section _____

Exercise 8-11

Requirement 1

<u>January 31</u>   <u>Debit</u>   <u>Credit</u>

_____   _____

                  _____   _____
                  _____   _____

                  _____

Requirement 2

<u>January 31</u>   <u>Debit</u>   <u>Credit</u>

_____   _____

                  _____   _____
                  _____   _____

                  _____

Exercise 8-12

Requirement 1

_____
_____

Requirement 2

_____
_____

Requirement 3

_____
_____

Exercise 8-12 Continued

Requirement 4

	Debit	Credit
_____	_____	
	_____	_____
	_____	

Exercise 8-13

Requirement 1

_____
_____
_____

	Debit	Credit
_____	_____	
	_____	_____
	_____	

Requirement 2

_____
_____
_____
_____
_____
_____
_____

	Debit	Credit
_____	_____	
	_____	_____
	_____	

Name _____ Date _____ Course _____ Section _____

Exercise 8-13 Continued

Requirement 3

_____
_____
_____
_____
_____

Requirement 4

_____
_____

Exercise 8-14

Requirement 1

_____
_____
_____
_____

Requirement 2

	Debit	Credit
_____	_____	
_____		_____
_____		

Requirement 3

	Debit	Credit
_____	_____	
_____		_____
_____		

Name _____ Date _____ Course _____ Section _____

Exercise 8-14 Continued

Warranty Liability

Exercise 8-15

Requirement 1

_____
_____
_____

Requirement 2

_____
_____

Requirement 3

	Debit	Credit

Exercise 8-16

Requirement 1

Current Ratio = [   ] = [   ] = [   ]

Acid-Test Ratio = [   ] = [   ] = [   ]

Requirement 2

_____
_____
_____
_____
_____
_____

Name _____ Date _____ Course _____ Section _____

Problem 8-1A

List A	List B
_____ 1. An IOU promising to repay the amount borrowed plus interest.	a. Recording of a loss contingency
_____ 2. Loss is reasonably possible and can be reasonably estimated.	b. Unearned revenues
_____ 3. Mixture of liabilities and equity a business uses.	c. The riskiness of a business's obligations
_____ 4. Loss is probable and can be reasonably estimated.	d. Disclosure of a loss contingency
_____ 5. A liability that requires the sacrifice of something other than cash.	e. Interest on debt
_____ 6. Long-term debt maturing within one year.	f. Payroll taxes
_____ 7. FICA and FUTA.	g. Line of credit
_____ 8. Informal agreement that permits a company to borrow up to a prearranged limit.	h. Capital structure
_____ 9. Classifying liabilities as either current or long-term helps investors and creditors assess this.	i. Notes payable
_____ 10. Amount of note payable **x** annual interest rate **x** fraction of the year.	j. Current portion of long-term debt

Problem 8-2A

Requirement 1

(a). <u>October 1, 2012</u>   <u>Debit</u>   <u>Credit</u>

_____   _____

            _____   _____

            _____   _____

(b). <u>October 1, 2012</u>

_____   _____

            _____   _____

            _____   _____

Name _____ Date _____ Course _____ Section _____

Problem 8-2A Continued

Requirement 2

(a). <u>December 31, 2012</u>   **Debit**   **Credit**

_____   _____   _____

         _____   _____   _____

         _____   _____   _____

(b). <u>December 31, 2012</u>

_____   _____   _____

         _____   _____   _____

         _____   _____   _____

Requirement 3

(a). <u>September 30, 2013</u>   **Debit**   **Credit**

_____   _____

_____   _____

_____   _____

         _____   _____   _____

         _____   _____   _____

(b). <u>September 30, 2013</u>

_____   _____

         _____   _____   _____

         _____   _____   _____

         _____   _____   _____

Name _____ Date _____ Course _____ Section _____

Problem 8-3A

Requirement 1

<u>January 31</u>   Debit   Credit

_____   _____

                            _____   _____
                            _____   _____
                            _____   _____
                            _____   _____

                    _____

Requirement 2

<u>January 31</u>   Debit   Credit

_____   _____

                            _____   _____
                            _____   _____

                    _____

Requirement 3

<u>January 31</u>   Debit   Credit

_____   _____

                            _____   _____
                            _____   _____

                    _____

Name _____ Date _____ Course _____ Section _____

Problem 8-4A

Requirement 1

<u>February 14</u>   Debit   Credit

_____   _____

                    _____   _____
                    _____   _____
                    _____   _____
                    _____   _____
                    _____   _____

                    _____

Requirement 2

<u>February 14</u>   Debit   Credit

_____   _____

                    _____   _____
                    _____   _____
                    _____   _____

                    _____

Requirement 3

<u>February 14</u>   Debit   Credit

_____   _____

                    _____   _____
                    _____   _____

                    _____

Name _____ Date _____ Course _____ Section _____

Problem 8-5A

Requirement 1

_____	=	$ _____ per season ticket	
_____	=	$ _____ per individual game ticket	

Requirement 2

	Debit	Credit
_____	_____	_____
_____	_____	_____
_____		

Requirement 3

	Debit	Credit
_____	_____	_____
_____	_____	_____
_____		

Problem 8-6A

Requirement 1

	Debit	Credit
_____	_____	_____
_____	_____	_____
_____		

Name _____ Date _____ Course _____ Section _____

Problem 8-6A Continued

	Debit	Credit
_____	_____	_____
_____	_____	_____
_____		

Requirement 2

Unearned Revenue

Problem 8-7A

Requirement 1

	Debit	Credit
_____	_____	_____
_____	_____	_____
_____	_____	_____

_____
_____
_____
_____

Requirement 2

	Debit	Credit
_____	_____	_____
_____	_____	_____
_____	_____	_____

Name _____ **Date** _____ **Course** _____ **Section** _____

Problem 8-7A Continued

_____
_____
_____
_____

Requirement 3

	Debit	Credit
_____	_____	_____
_____	_____	_____
_____		

_____
_____

Problem 8-8A

Requirement 1

	Debit	Credit
_____	_____	_____
_____	_____	_____
_____		

_____
_____
_____
_____
_____

 Financial Accounting

Name _____ **Date** _____ **Course** _____ **Section** _____

Problem 8-8A Continued

Requirement 2

	Debit	Credit
_____		
_____	_____	
	_____	_____
	_____	
_____		
_____		
_____		
_____		
_____		

Requirement 3

	Debit	Credit
_____		
	_____	
	_____	_____
	_____	
_____		
_____		
_____		
_____		
_____		

 Financial Accounting

Name _____ Date _____ Course _____ Section _____

Problem 8-9A

Requirement 1

	Home Depot	Lowe's
Current Ratio =	=	

_____
_____
_____
_____
_____
_____

Requirement 2

	Home Depot	Lowe's
Current Ratio =	=	
	=	

_____
_____
_____
_____
_____
_____

Requirement 3

_____
_____
_____
_____
_____
_____
_____
_____
_____

Name _____ Date _____ Course _____ Section _____

Problem 8-1B

List A	List B
_____ 1. Interest expense is recorded in the period interest is incurred rather than in the period interest is paid.	a. The riskiness of a business's obligations
_____ 2. Loss is reasonably possible and can be reasonably estimated.	b. Current portion of long-term debt
_____ 3. Cash, short-term investments, and accounts receivable all divided by current liabilities.	c. Recording a loss contingency
_____ 4. Loss is probable and can be reasonably estimated.	d. Disclosure of a loss contingency
_____ 5. Gift certificates.	e. Interest expense
_____ 6. Long-term debt maturing within one year.	f. FICA
_____ 7. Social Security and Medicare.	g. Commercial paper
_____ 8. Unsecured notes sold in minimum denominations of $25,000 with maturities up to 270 days.	h. Acid-test ratio
_____ 9. Classifying liabilities as either current or long-term helps investors and creditors assess this.	i. Accrual accounting
_____ 10. Incurred on a notes payable.	j. Unearned revenues

Problem 8-2B

Requirement 1

(a). <u>November 1, 2012</u>   **Debit**   **Credit**

_____   _____

_____   _____

(b). <u>November 1, 2012</u>

_____   _____

_____   _____

_____

Name _____ Date _____ Course _____ Section _____

Problem 8-2B Continued

Requirement 2

(a). <u>December 31, 2012</u>   **Debit**   **Credit**

_____   _____

                    _____   _____

                    _____

(b). <u>December 31, 2012</u>

_____   _____

                    _____   _____

                    _____

Requirement 3

(a). <u>April 30, 2013</u>   **Debit**   **Credit**

_____   _____
_____   _____
_____   _____

                    _____   _____

                    _____

(b). <u>April 30, 2013</u>

_____   _____

                    _____   _____
                    _____   _____
                    _____   _____

                    _____

Name _____ Date _____ Course _____ Section _____

Problem 8-3B

Requirement 1

<u>January 31</u>   **Debit**   **Credit**

_____   _____

                              _____   _____
                              _____   _____
                              _____   _____
                              _____   _____

                              _____

Requirement 2

<u>January 31</u>   **Debit**   **Credit**

_____   _____

                              _____   _____
                              _____   _____

                              _____

Requirement 3

<u>January 31</u>   **Debit**   **Credit**

_____   _____

                              _____   _____
                              _____   _____

                              _____

The McGraw-Hill Companies   *Financial Accounting*

Name _____ Date _____ Course _____ Section _____

Problem 8-4B

Requirement 1

<u>January 24</u>   Debit   Credit

_____   _____

                          _____   _____
                          _____   _____
                          _____   _____
                          _____   _____
                          _____   _____

                  _____

Requirement 2

<u>January 24</u>   Debit   Credit

_____   _____

                          _____   _____
                          _____   _____
                          _____   _____
                          _____   _____

                  _____

Requirement 3

<u>January 24</u>   Debit   Credit

_____   _____

                          _____   _____
                          _____   _____

                  _____

Name _____ Date _____ Course _____ Section _____

Problem 8-5B

Requirement 1

		=		
		=	$ _____ per season ticket	
		=	$ _____ per individual game ticket	

Requirement 2

	Debit	Credit
_____	_____	
_____		_____
_____		

Requirement 3

	Debit	Credit
_____	_____	
_____		_____
_____		

Problem 8-6B

Requirement 1

	Debit	Credit
_____	_____	
_____		_____
_____		

The McGraw-Hill Companies   *Financial Accounting*

Name _____ Date _____ Course _____ Section _____

Problem 8-6B Continued

Requirement 2

	Debit	Credit
_____	_____	
_____		_____
_____		_____
_____		

Requirement 3

Unearned Revenue

Problem 8-7B

Requirement 1

	Debit	Credit
_____	_____	
_____		_____
_____		

_____

_____

_____

Requirement 2

	Debit	Credit
_____	_____	
_____		_____
_____		

Name _____ Date _____ Course _____ Section _____

Problem 8-7B Continued

_____
_____
_____

Requirement 3

	Debit	Credit

_____   _____
          _____   _____
          _____   _____

_____
_____
_____

Requirement 4

	Debit	Credit

_____   _____
          _____   _____
          _____   _____

_____
_____
_____
_____

Name _____ Date _____ Course _____ Section _____

Problem 8-8B

Requirement 1

	Debit	Credit
_____	_____	_____
_____	_____	_____
_____	_____	

_____
_____
_____
_____
_____
_____

Requirement 2

	Debit	Credit
_____	_____	_____
_____	_____	_____
_____	_____	

_____
_____
_____
_____
_____

Requirement 3

	Debit	Credit
_____	_____	
_____	_____	_____
_____		

_____
_____
_____
_____
_____

The McGraw-Hill Companies *Financial Accounting*

Name _____ Date _____ Course _____ Section _____

Problem 8-9B

Requirement 1

	American	Delta

Current Ratio = [_____] = [_____] [_____]

= [_____] [_____]

_____
_____
_____
_____
_____
_____

Requirement 2

	American	Delta

Current Ratio = [_____] = [_____] [_____]

= [_____] [_____]

_____
_____
_____
_____
_____

Requirement 3

_____
_____
_____
_____
_____
_____
_____
_____
_____

Name _____ Date _____ Course _____ Section _____

Exercise 9-1

Requirement 1

	Issue Bonds	Issue Stock
Operating income		
Interest expense		
Income before tax		
Income tax expense (30%)		
Net income		
# of shares		
Earnings per share		

Requirement 2

_____

_____

_____

Exercise 9-2

Terms

_____ 1. Bond indenture.
_____ 2. Secured bond.
_____ 3. Unsecured bond.
_____ 4. Term bond.
_____ 5. Serial bond.
_____ 6. Callable bond.
_____ 7. Convertible bond.
_____ 8. Bond issue costs.

Definitions

(a) Allows the issuer to pay off the bonds early at a fixed price.
(b) Matures in installments.
(c) Secured only by the "full faith and credit" of the issuing corporation.
(d) Allows the investor to transfer each bond into shares of common stock.
(e) A contract between the issuer and the investor.
(f) Matures on a single date.
(g) Supported by specific assets pledged as collateral by the issuer.
(h) Includes underwriting, legal, accounting, registration, and printing fees.

Name _____ Date _____ Course _____ Section _____

Exercise 9-3

Requirement 1

Bonds issued at : _____
Issue price is : _____

Calculator Input		
Bond Characteristics	**Key**	**Amount**
1. Face amount	FV	
2. Interest payment	PMT	
3. Market interest rate	I	
4. Periods to maturity	N	

Calculator Output		
Issue price	**PV**	

Requirement 2

Bonds issued at : _____
Issue price is : _____

Calculator Input		
Bond Characteristics	**Key**	**Amount**
1. Face amount	FV	
2. Interest payment	PMT	
3. Market interest rate	I	
4. Periods to maturity	N	

Calculator Output		
Issue price	**PV**	

Name _____ Date _____ Course _____ Section _____

Exercise 9-3 Continued

Requirement 3

Bonds issued at : _____
Issue price is : _____

Calculator Input		
Bond Characteristics	**Key**	**Amount**
1. Face amount	FV	
2. Interest payment	PMT	
3. Market interest rate	I	
4. Periods to maturity	N	

Calculator Output		
Issue price	**PV**	

Exercise 9-4

Requirement 1

Bonds issued at : _____
Issue price is : _____

Calculator Input		
Bond Characteristics	**Key**	**Amount**
1. Face amount	FV	
2. Interest payment	PMT	
3. Market interest rate	I	
4. Periods to maturity	N	

Calculator Output		
Issue price	**PV**	

Name _____ Date _____ Course _____ Section _____

Exercise 9-4 Continued

Requirement 2

Bonds issued at : _____
Issue price is : _____

Calculator Input		
Bond Characteristics	**Key**	**Amount**
1. Face amount	FV	
2. Interest payment	PMT	
3. Market interest rate	I	
4. Periods to maturity	N	

Calculator Output		
Issue price	**PV**	

Requirement 3

Bonds issued at : _____
Issue price is : _____

Calculator Input		
Bond Characteristics	**Key**	**Amount**
1. Face amount	FV	
2. Interest payment	PMT	
3. Market interest rate	I	
4. Periods to maturity	N	

Calculator Output		
Issue price	**PV**	

Name _____ Date _____ Course _____ Section _____

Exercise 9-5

January 1, 2012   **Debit**   **Credit**

_____   _____

     _____   _____

     _____   _____

June 30, 2012

_____   _____

     _____   _____

     _____

December 31, 2012

_____   _____

     _____   _____

     _____

Exercise 9-6

Requirement 1

Date	Cash Paid	Interest Expense	Increase in Carrying value	Carrying Value
01/01/12				
06/30/12	_____	_____	_____	_____
12/31/12	_____	_____	_____	_____

Name _____ Date _____ Course _____ Section _____

Exercise 9-6 Continued

Requirement 2

<u>January 1, 2012</u>   Debit _____   Credit _____

_____   _____

                      _____   _____

                      _____

<u>June 30, 2012</u>

                                                                _____

_____

                      _____   _____

                      _____   _____

                      _____

<u>December 31, 2012</u>

_____   _____

                      _____   _____

                      _____   _____

                      _____

Exercise 9-7

Requirement 1

Date	Cash Paid	Interest Expense	Decrease in Carrying value	Carrying Value
01/01/12				
06/30/12	_____	_____	_____	_____
12/31/12	_____	_____	_____	_____

Name _____ Date _____ Course _____ Section _____

Exercise 9-7 Continued

Requirement 2

<u>January 1, 2012</u>   Debit   Credit

_____   _____

               _____   _____

               _____

<u>June 30, 2012</u>

_____   _____

_____   _____

               _____   _____

               _____

<u>December 31, 2012</u>

_____   _____

_____

               _____   _____

               _____

Exercise 9-8

<u>January 1, 2012</u>   Debit   Credit

_____   _____

               _____   _____

               _____

Name _____ Date _____ Course _____ Section _____

Exercise 9-8 Continued

<u>June 30, 2012</u>   Debit   Credit

_____   _____   _____

        _____   _____   _____

        _____   _____

<u>December 31, 2012</u>

_____   _____

        _____   _____   _____

        _____   _____

Exercise 9-9

Requirement 1

Date	Cash Paid	Interest Expense	Increase in Carrying value	Carrying Value
01/01/12	_____			_____
06/30/12	_____	_____	_____	_____
12/31/12	_____	_____	_____	_____

Requirement 2

<u>January 1, 2012</u>   Debit   Credit

_____   _____   _____

        _____   _____   _____

        _____   _____

Name _____ Date _____ Course _____ Section _____

Exercise 9-9 Continued

June 30, 2012   **Debit**   **Credit**

_____   _____   _____

      _____   _____

      _____

December 31, 2012

_____   _____

      _____   _____

      _____

Exercise 9-10

Requirement 1

Date	Cash Paid	Interest Expense	Decrease in Carrying value	Carrying Value
01/01/12				
06/30/12				
12/31/12				

Requirement 2

January 1, 2012   **Debit**   **Credit**

_____   _____   _____

      _____   _____

      _____

Name _____ Section _____ Date _____ Course _____ Section _____

Exercise 9-10 Continued

June 30, 2012   ___Debit___   ___Credit___

_____   _____

_____   _____

            _____   _____

                        _____

December 31, 2012

_____   _____

_____   _____

            _____   _____

                        _____

Exercise 9-11

January 1, 2012   ___Debit___   ___Credit___

_____   _____

            _____   _____

                        _____

June 30, 2012

_____   _____

            _____   _____

                        _____

December 31, 2012

_____   _____

            _____   _____

                        _____

Name _____ Date _____ Course _____ Section _____

Exercise 9-12

Requirement 1

Date	Cash Paid	Interest Expense	Increase in Carrying value	Carrying Value
01/01/12	_____	_____	_____	_____
12/31/12	_____	_____	_____	_____
12/31/13	_____	_____	_____	_____

Requirement 2

<u>January 1, 2012</u>	Debit	Credit
_____	_____	
_____	_____	_____
_____		_____

<u>December 31, 2012</u>		
_____	_____	
_____	_____	_____
_____	_____	_____
_____	_____	

<u>December 31, 2013</u>		
_____	_____	
_____	_____	_____
_____	_____	_____
_____	_____	

The McGraw-Hill Companies *Financial Accounting*

Name _____ Date _____ Course _____ Section _____

Exercise 9-13

Requirement 1

Date	Cash Paid	Interest Expense	Decrease in Carrying value	Carrying Value
01/01/12				
12/31/12	_____	_____	_____	_____
12/31/13	_____	_____	_____	_____

Requirement 2

<u>January 1, 2012</u>   Debit   Credit

_____   _____

_____   _____

_____   _____

<u>December 31, 2012</u>

_____   _____

_____   _____

_____   _____

_____

<u>December 31, 2013</u>

_____   _____

_____   _____

_____   _____

_____

Name _____ Date _____ Course _____ Section _____

Exercise 9-14

Requirement 1

Date	Cash Paid	Interest Expense	Increase in Carrying value	Carrying Value
01/01/12	_____	_____	_____	_____
06/30/12	_____	_____	_____	_____
12/31/12	_____	_____	_____	_____
06/30/13	_____	_____	_____	_____
12/31/13	_____	_____	_____	_____

Requirement 2

Calculator Input		
Bond Characteristic	Key	Amount
1. Face amount	FV	
2. Interest payment each period	PMT	
3. Market interest rate each period	I	
4. Periods to maturity	N	

Calculator Output		
Issue Price	PV	

<u>December 31, 2013</u>   Debit   Credit

_____   _____

_____   _____

_____   _____

_____   _____

Name _____ Date _____ Course _____ Section _____

Exercise 9-15

Requirement 1

Date	Cash Paid	Interest Expense	Decrease in Carrying value	Carrying Value
01/01/12	_____	_____	_____	_____
06/30/12	_____	_____	_____	_____
12/31/12	_____	_____	_____	_____
06/30/13	_____	_____	_____	_____
12/31/13	_____	_____	_____	_____
06/30/14	_____	_____	_____	_____
12/31/14	_____	_____	_____	_____

Requirement 2

Calculator Input		
Bond Characteristic	Key	Amount
1. Face amount	FV	
2. Interest payment each period	PMT	
3. Market interest rate each period	I	
4. Periods to maturity	N	

Calculator Output		
Issue Price	PV	

December 31, 2012   Debit   Credit

_____   _____

     _____   _____

     _____   _____

     _____

Name _____ Date _____ Course _____ Section _____

Exercise 9-16

Requirement 1

<u>January 1, 2012</u>   Debit   Credit

_____   _____

_____   _____

_____

<u>January 31, 2012</u>

_____   _____

_____   _____

_____   _____

_____

<u>February 28, 2012</u>

_____   _____

_____   _____

_____   _____

_____

Exercise 9-17

Requirement 1

		÷		=	Debt to Equity Ratio
Expedia		÷		=	
Priceline		÷		=	

Name _____ Date _____ Course _____ Section _____

Exercise 9-17 Continued

_____
_____
_____
_____

Requirement 2

		÷		=	Debt to Equity Ratio
Expedia		÷		=	
Priceline		÷		=	

_____
_____
_____
_____
_____
_____

Name _____ Date _____ Course _____ Section _____

Problem 9-1A

Requirement 1

Calculator Input		
Bond Characteristic	**Key**	**Amount**
1. Face amount	FV	
2. Interest payment each period	PMT	
3. Market interest rate each period	I	
4. Periods to maturity	N	

Calculator Output		
Issue Price	**PV**	

Date	Cash Paid	Interest Expense	Increase in Carrying value	Carrying Value
01/01/12				
06/30/12	_____	_____	_____	_____
12/31/12	_____	_____	_____	_____

Requirement 2

Calculator Input		
Bond Characteristic	**Key**	**Amount**
1. Face amount	FV	
2. Interest payment each period	PMT	
3. Market interest rate each period	I	
4. Periods to maturity	N	

Calculator Output		
Issue Price	**PV**	

Name _____ Date _____ Course _____ Section _____

Problem 9-1A Continued

Date	Cash Paid	Interest Expense	Increase in Carrying value	Carrying Value
01/01/12	_____	_____	_____	_____
06/30/12	_____	_____	_____	_____
12/31/12	_____	_____	_____	_____

Requirement 3

Calculator Input		
Bond Characteristics	Key	Amount
1. Face amount	FV	
2. Interest payment	PMT	
3. Market interest rate	I	
4. Periods to maturity	N	

Calculator Output		
Issue Price	PV	

Date	Cash Paid	Interest Expense	Decrease in Carrying value	Carrying Value
01/01/12	_____	_____	_____	_____
06/30/12	_____	_____	_____	_____
12/31/12	_____	_____	_____	_____

 Financial Accounting

Name _____ Date _____ Course _____ Section _____

Problem 9-2A

Requirement 1

<u>January 1, 2012</u>   Debit   Credit

_____   _____

_____   _____

_____

<u>June 30, 2012</u>

_____   _____

_____   _____

_____

<u>December 31, 2012</u>

_____   _____

_____   _____

_____

Requirement 2

<u>January 1, 2012</u>   Debit   Credit

_____   _____

_____   _____

_____

<u>June 30, 2012</u>

_____   _____

_____   _____

_____

_____

The McGraw-Hill Companies   *Financial Accounting*

Name _____ Date _____ Course _____ Section _____

Problem 9-2A Continued

December 31, 2012   Debit   Credit

_____   _____   _____

                    _____   _____

                    _____   _____

                    _____

Requirement 3

January 1, 2012   Debit   Credit

_____   _____   _____

                    _____   _____

                    _____

June 30, 2012

_____   _____   _____

_____   _____   _____

                    _____

December 31, 2012

_____   _____   _____

_____   _____   _____

                    _____   _____

                    _____

Name _____ Date _____ Course _____ Section _____

Problem 9-3A

1. _____
2. _____
3. _____
4. _____
5. _____
6. _____
7. _____

Problem 9-4A

Requirement 1

Date	Cash Paid	Interest Expense	Increase in Carrying value	Carrying Value
01/01/12				
06/30/12				
12/31/12				

Requirement 2

January 1, 2012 _____   **Debit**   **Credit**

_____   _____   _____

_____   _____   _____

Requirement 3

June 30, 2012 _____   **Debit**   **Credit**

_____   _____   _____

_____   _____   _____

_____   _____   _____

Name _____ Date _____ Course _____ Section _____

Problem 9-4A Continued

<u>December 31, 2012</u>   Debit   Credit

_____ _____ _____

_____ _____ _____

_____ _____ _____

_____

Problem 9-5A

Requirement 1

<u>January 1, 2012</u> _____   Debit   Credit

_____ _____

_____ _____ _____

_____ _____ _____

_____

Requirement 2

Date	Cash Paid	Interest Expense	Increase in Carrying value	Carrying Value
01/01/12	_____	_____	_____	_____
01/31/12	_____	_____	_____	_____
02/28/12	_____	_____	_____	_____

Name _____ Date _____ Course _____ Section _____

Problem 9-5A Continued

Requirement 3

<u>January 1, 2012</u>   Debit   Credit

_____   _____

_____   _____

            _____   _____

            _____

_____
_____
_____

Requirement 4

_____
_____
_____
_____
_____

Problem 9-6A

Requirement 1

Assets	=		+	
	=		+	

_____
_____
_____

Requirement 2

	÷		=	Debt to Equity Ratio
	÷		=	

Name _____ Date _____ Course _____ Section _____

Problem 9-6A Continued

Requirement 3

_____
_____
_____
_____
_____
_____
_____

Requirement 4

_____
_____
_____
_____
_____
_____

Requirement 5

_____
_____
_____
_____
_____
_____

Operating lease :					
	÷		=		**Debt to Equity Ratio**
	÷		=		

Capital lease :					
	÷		=		**Debt to Equity Ratio**
	÷		=		

 Financial Accounting

Name _____ Date _____ Course _____ Section _____

Problem 9-7A

Requirement 1

		÷		=	Debt to Equity
Starwood		÷		=	
Marriot		÷		=	

_____

_____

_____

Requirement 2

		÷		=	Return on Assets Ratio
Starwood		÷		=	
Marriot		÷		=	

		÷		=	Return on Equity Ratio
Starwood		÷		=	
Marriot		÷		=	

_____

_____

Requirement 3

		÷		=	Times Interest Earned Ratio
Starwood		÷		=	
Marriot		÷		=	

_____

_____

_____

_____

_____

Name _____ Date _____ Course _____ Section _____

Problem 9-1B

Requirement 1

Calculator Input		
Bond Characteristics	**Key**	**Amount**
1. Face amount	FV	
2. Interest payment	PMT	
3. Market interest rate	I	
4. Periods to maturity	N	

Calculator Output		
Issue price	**PV**	

Date	Cash Paid	Interest Expense	Increase in Carrying value	Carrying Value

Requirement 2

Calculator Input		
Bond Characteristics	**Key**	**Amount**
1. Face amount	FV	
2. Interest payment	PMT	
3. Market interest rate	I	
4. Periods to maturity	N	

Calculator Output		
Issue price	**PV**	

The McGraw-Hill Companies   *Financial Accounting*

Name _____ Date _____ Course _____ Section _____

Problem 9-1B Continued

Date	Cash Paid	Interest Expense	Increase in Carrying value	Carrying Value

Requirement 3

Bonds issued at : _____

Issue price is : _____

Calculator Input		
Bond Characteristics	**Key**	**Amount**
1. Face amount	FV	
2. Interest payment	PMT	
3. Market interest rate	I	
4. Periods to maturity	N	

Calculator Output		
Issue price	**PV**	

Date	Cash Paid	Interest Expense	Increase in Carrying value	Carrying Value

Name _____ Date _____ Course _____ Section _____

Problem 9-2B

Requirement 1

<u>January 1, 2012</u>   Debit   Credit

_____   _____   _____

          _____   _____

          _____

<u>June 30, 2012</u>

_____   _____

          _____   _____

          _____

<u>December 31, 2012</u>

_____   _____

          _____   _____

Requirement 2

<u>January 1, 2012</u>   Debit   Credit

_____   _____   _____

          _____   _____

          _____

<u>June 30, 2012</u>

_____   _____

          _____   _____

          _____   _____

          _____

                             Financial Accounting

Name _____ **Date** _____ **Course** _____ **Section** _____

Problem 9-2B Continued

December 31, 2012	Debit	Credit
_____	_____	
	_____	_____
	_____	_____
	_____	

Requirement 3

January 1, 2012	Debit	Credit
_____	_____	
	_____	_____
	_____	

June 30, 2012

	Debit	Credit
_____	_____	
_____	_____	
	_____	_____
	_____	

December 31, 2012

	Debit	Credit
_____	_____	
_____	_____	
	_____	_____
	_____	

 Financial Accounting

Name _____ **Date** _____ **Course** _____ **Section** _____

Problem 9-3B

1. _____
2. _____
3. _____
4. _____
5. _____
6. _____
7. _____

Problem 9-4B

Requirement 1

Date	Cash Paid	Interest Expense	Decrease in Carrying value	Carrying Value
01/01/12	_____	_____	_____	_____
06/30/12	_____	_____	_____	_____
12/31/12	_____	_____	_____	_____

Requirement 2

January 1, 2012

	Debit	Credit
_____	_____	
		_____
_____		

Requirement 3

June 30, 2012

	Debit	Credit
_____	_____	
_____	_____	
		_____
_____		

Name _____ Date _____ Course _____ Section _____

Problem 9-4B Continued

<u>December 31, 2012</u>   **Debit**   **Credit**

_____   _____

_____   _____

                 _____   _____

                 _____   _____

Problem 9-5B

Requirement 1

<u>January 01, 2012</u>   **Debit**   **Credit**

_____   _____

                 _____   _____

                 _____   _____

                 _____   _____

Requirement 2

Date	Cash Paid	Interest Expense	Decrease in Carrying value	Carrying Value
01/01/12				
01/31/12	_____	_____	_____	_____
02/28/12	_____	_____	_____	_____
	_____	_____	_____	_____

The McGraw-Hill Companies   *Financial Accounting*

Name _____ Date _____ Course _____ Section _____

Problem 9-5B Continued

Requirement 3

<u>January 31, 2012</u>   Debit   Credit

_____   _____

_____   _____

                    _____   _____

                    _____

_____
_____
_____
_____
_____
_____

Requirement 4

_____
_____
_____
_____
_____

Problem 9-6B

Requirement 1

Assets	=		+	
	=		+	

Requirement 2

	÷		=	Debt to Equity Ratio
	÷		=	

The McGraw-Hill Companies   *Financial Accounting*

Name _____ Date _____ Course _____ Section _____

Problem 9-6B Continued

Requirement 3

_____
_____
_____
_____
_____
_____
_____
_____
_____

Requirement 4

_____
_____
_____
_____
_____
_____

Requirement 5

_____
_____
_____
_____
_____

Operating lease :					
	÷			=	**Debt to Equity Ratio**
	÷			=	

Capital lease :					
	÷			=	**Debt to Equity Ratio**
	÷			=	

Name _____ Date _____ Course _____ Section _____

Problem 9-7B

Requirement 1

	÷		=	**Debt to Equity Ratio**
Royal Caribbean	÷		=	
Carnival	÷		=	

_____
_____
_____
_____
_____

Requirement 2

	÷		=	**Return on Assets Ratio**
Royal Caribbean	÷		=	
Carnival	÷		=	

	÷		=	**Return on Equity Ratio**
Royal Caribbean	÷		=	
Carnival	÷		=	

_____
_____
_____
_____
_____

Name _____ Date _____ Course _____ Section _____

Problem 9-7B Continued

Requirement 3

	÷		=	Return on Assets Ratio
Royal Caribbean	÷		=	
Carnival	÷		=	
	÷		=	

_____

_____

_____

_____

_____

_____

The McGraw-Hill Companies *Financial Accounting*

Name _____ Date _____ Course _____ Section _____

Exercise 10-1

Terms

_____ 1. Publicly held corporation
_____ 2. Model Business Corporation Act
_____ 3. Articles of Incorporation
_____ 4. Limited liability
_____ 5. Mutual agency
_____ 6. Double taxation
_____ 7. S Corporation
_____ 8. Limited liability corporation

Definitions

a. Shareholders can lose no more than the amount they invest in the company.
b. Corporate earnings are taxed twice - at the corporate level and individual shareholder level.
c. Like an S corporation, but there are no limitations on the number of owners as in an S corporation.
d. Designed to serve as a guide to states in the development of their corporate statutes.
e. Allows for legal treatment as a corporation, but tax treatment as a partnership.
f. Has stock traded on a stock exchange such as the New York Stock Exchange (NYSE).
g. Individual partners in a partnership have the power to bind the business to a contract.
h. Describe (a) the nature of the firm's business activities, (b) the shares to be issued, and (c) the composition of the initial board of directors

Exercise 10-2

Authorized stock :

_____
_____
_____
_____

Issued stock :

_____
_____
_____

Outstanding stock :

_____
_____
_____
_____

Name _____ Date _____ Course _____ Section _____

Exercise 10-2 Continued

Preferred stock :

_____

_____

_____

_____

_____

Treasury stock :

_____

_____

_____

Exercise 10-3

Requirement 1

January 1, 2012   Debit   Credit

_____   _____   _____

                    _____   _____

                    _____   _____

April 1, 2012

_____   _____

                    _____   _____

                    _____   _____

Requirement 2

January 1, 2012   Debit   Credit

_____   _____

                    _____   _____

                    _____   _____

                    _____

Name _____ Date _____ Course _____ Section _____

Exercise 10-3 Continued

<u>April 1, 2012</u>   **Debit**   **Credit**

_____   _____

     _____   _____

     _____   _____

     _____

Requirement 3

<u>January 1, 2012</u>   **Debit**   **Credit**

_____   _____

     _____   _____

     _____   _____

     _____

<u>April 1, 2012</u>

_____   _____

     _____   _____

     _____   _____

     _____

Exercise 10-4

Requirement 1

Name _____ Date _____ Course _____ Section _____

Exercise 10-4 Continued

Requirement 2

Exercise 10-5

February 1

	Debit	Credit
_____	____	
_____		____
_____		

May 15

_____	____	
_____		____
_____		____
_____		

October 1

_____	____	
_____		____
_____		

October 15

_____	____	
_____		____
_____		

Name _____ Date _____ Course _____ Section _____

Exercise 10-5 Continued

October 31   <u>Debit</u>   <u>Credit</u>

_____

                    _____   _____

                    _____   _____

Exercise 10-6

January 2, 2012   <u>Debit</u>   <u>Credit</u>

_____   _____   _____

                    _____   _____

                    _____   _____

                    _____

February 6, 2012

_____   _____   _____

                    _____   _____

                    _____   _____

                    _____

September 10, 2012

_____   _____   _____

                    _____   _____

                    _____

December 15, 2012

_____   _____   _____

                    _____   _____

                    _____   _____

                    _____

Name _____ Date _____ Course _____ Section _____

Exercise 10-7

Finishing Touches Balance Sheet (Stockholders' Equity Section) December 31, 2012	
Stockholders' equity:	
Total paid-in capital	
Total stockholders' equity	

Exercise 10-8

March 15	Debit	Credit
_____	_____	
_____		_____
_____		

March 30		
_____	_____	
_____		_____
_____		

April 13		
_____	_____	
_____		_____
_____		

Name _____ Date _____ Course _____ Section _____

Exercise 10-9

	Debit	Credit
March 1, 2012		
_____ _____		
_____		_____
_____		_____
_____		
May 10, 2012		
_____ _____	_____	
_____		_____
_____		
June 1, 2012		
_____ _____		
_____		_____
_____		
July 1, 2012		
_____ _____	_____	
_____		_____
_____		
October 21, 2012		
_____ _____	_____	
_____		_____
_____		_____
_____		

Name _____ Date _____ Course _____ Section _____

Exercise 10-10

Power Drive Corportation Balance Sheet (Stockholders' Equity Section) December 31, 2012	
Stockholders' equity:	
Total paid-in capital	
Total stockholders' equity	

Exercise 10-11

	Common Stock	Additional Paid-in Capital	Retained Earnings	Treasury Stock	Total Stockholders' Equity
Power Drive Corporation **Statement of Stockholders' Equity** **For the Year Ended December 31, 2012**					
Balance, January 1	_____	_____	_____	_____	_____
	_____	_____			_____
				_____	_____
			_____		_____
	_____	_____	_____	_____	_____
Balance, December 31	_____	_____	_____	_____	_____

Name _____ Date _____ Course _____ Section _____

Exercise 10-12

Transaction	Total Assets	Total Liabilities	Total Stockholders' Equity
Issue common stock	_____	_____	_____
Issue preferred stock	_____	_____	_____
Purchase treasury stock	_____	_____	_____
Sale of treasury stock	_____	_____	_____
Declare cash dividend	_____	_____	_____
Pay cash dividend	_____	_____	_____
100% stock dividend	_____	_____	_____
2-for-1 stock split	_____	_____	_____

Exercise 10-13

United Apparel Balance Sheet (Stockholders' Equity Section) December 31, 2012	
Stockholders' equity:	
Total paid-in capital	
Total stockholders' equity	

Exercise 10-14

Requirement 1

		÷		=	**Return on Equity**
		÷		=	
Limited Brands		÷		=	

_____

_____

Name _____ Date _____ Course _____ Section _____

Exercise 10-14 Continued

Requirement 2

		÷		=	Return on the Market Value of Equity
Limited Brands		÷		=	

_____
_____
_____

Requirement 3

		÷		=	Earnings Per Share
Limited Brands		÷		=	

_____
_____
_____
_____

Requirement 4

		÷		=	Price-Earnings Ratio
Limited Brands		÷		=	

_____
_____
_____

Exercise 10-15

Requirement 1

		÷		=	Earnings Per Share
2011		÷		=	
2012		÷		=	

_____
_____

Name _____ Date _____ Course _____ Section _____

Exercise 10-15 Continued

Requirement 2

		÷		=	**Price-Earnings Ratio**
2011		÷		=	
2012		÷		=	

_____

_____

The McGraw-Hill Companies

Financial Accounting

Problem 10-1A

<u>Terms</u>

_____	1.	Cumulative
_____	2.	Retained earnings
_____	3.	Outstanding stock
_____	4.	Limited liability
_____	5.	Treasury stock
_____	6.	Issued stock
_____	7.	Angel investors
_____	8.	Paid-in capital
_____	9.	Authorized stock
_____	10.	Redeemable

<u>Definitions</u>

a. The amount invested by stockholders.

b. Shares available to sell.

c. Shares can be returned to the corporation at a predetermined price.

d. The earnings not paid out in dividends.

e. Shares actually sold.

f. Shares receive priority for future dividends if dividends are not paid in a given year.

g. Shares held by investors.

h. Shareholders can lose no more than the amount they invested in the company.

i. Wealthy individuals in the business community willing to risk investment funds on a promising business venture.

j. The corporation's own stock that it reacquired.

Name _____ Date _____ Course _____ Section _____

Problem 10-2A

Requirement 1

<u>March 1, 2012</u>

	Debit	Credit
_____	_____	
_____		_____
_____		_____
_____		

<u>May 15, 2012</u>

_____	_____	
_____		_____
_____		

<u>July 10, 2012</u>

_____	_____	
_____		_____
_____		_____
_____		

<u>October 15, 2012</u>

_____	_____	
_____		_____
_____		_____

<u>December 1, 2012</u>

_____	_____	
_____		_____
_____		

Name _____ Date _____ Course _____ Section _____

Problem 10-2A Continued

December 31, 2012	Debit	Credit
_____	_____	_____
_____	_____	_____
_____		

Requirement 2

Transaction	Total Assets	Total Liabilities	Total Stockholders' Equity
Issue common stock			
Repurchase treasury stock			
Reissue treasury stock			
Issue preferred stock			
Declare cash dividends			
Pay cash dividends			

Problem 10-3A

Requirement 1

	Before	After 100% Stock Dividend	After 2-for-1 Stock Split
Common stock, $1 par value			
Additional paid-in capital			
Total paid-in capital			
Retained Earnings			
Total stockholders' equity			
Shares outstanding			
Par value per share			
Share price			

Name _____ Date _____ Course _____ Section _____

Problem 10-3A Continued

Requirement 2

_____
_____
_____
_____
_____

Problem 10-4A

Requirement 1

_____
_____

Requirement 2

_____
_____

Requirement 3

_____
_____
_____
_____
_____
_____

Requirement 4

Retained Earnings, Beginning	
Retained Earnings, Ending	

Requirement 5

_____
_____
_____
_____

Name _____ Date _____ Course _____ Section _____

Problem 10-5A

Requirement 1

Donnie Hilfiger Balance Sheet (Stockholders' Equity Section) December 31, 2012	
Stockholders' equity:	
Total paid-in capital	
Total stockholders' equity	

Requirement 2

	Donnie Hilfiger Statement of Stockholders' Equity For the Year Ended December 31, 2012					
	Preferred Stock	**Common Stock**	**Additional Paid-in Capital**	**Retained Earnings**	**Treasury Stock**	**Total Stockholders' Equity**
Balance, January 1						
Issued common stock						
Purchased treasury stock						
Sale of treasury stock						
Issued preferred stock						
Cash dividends						
Net income						
Balance, December 31						

Name _____ Date _____ Course _____ Section _____

Problem 10-5A Continued

Requirement 3

_____

_____

_____

_____

_____

_____

_____

_____

Problem 10-6A

Requirement 1

January 2, 2012   Debit   Credit

_____   _____

                    _____   _____

                    _____   _____

                    _____

February 14, 2012

_____

                    _____   _____

                    _____   _____

                    _____

May 8, 2012

_____   _____

                    _____   _____

                    _____

The McGraw-Hill Companies   *Financial Accounting*

Name _____ Date _____ Course _____ Section _____

Problem 10-6A Continued

May 31, 2012	Debit	Credit
_____	_____	_____
_____	_____	
_____	_____	
_____		

December 1, 2012

	Debit	Credit
_____	_____	
_____	_____	_____
_____		

December 30, 2012

	Debit	Credit
_____	_____	
_____	_____	_____
_____		

Requirement 2

Major League Apparel Balance Sheet (Stockholders' Equity Section) December 31, 2012	
Stockholders' equity:	
Total paid-in capital	
Total stockholders' equity	

Name _____ Date _____ Course _____ Section _____

Problem 10-7A

Requirement 1

		÷		=	**Return on Equity**
Abercrombie		÷		=	

_____

_____

_____

Requirement 2

		÷		=	**Return on the Market Value of Equity**
Abercrombie		÷		=	

_____

_____

_____

Requirement 3

_____

_____

_____

_____

_____

_____

_____

_____

Requirement 4

		÷		=	**Price-Earnings Ratio**
Abercrombie		÷		=	

_____

_____

_____

_____

Name _____ Date _____ Course _____ Section _____

Problem 10-1B

<u>Terms</u>

_____	1. PE ratio
_____	2. Stockholders' equity section of the balance sheet
_____	3. Accumulated deficit
_____	4. Growth stocks
_____	5. 100% stock dividend
_____	6. Statement of stockholders' equity
_____	7. Treasury stock
_____	8. Value stocks
_____	9. Return on equity
_____	10. Retained earnings

<u>Definitions</u>

a. A debit balance in retained earnings.

b. Priced high in relation to current earnings as investors expect future earnings to be higher.

c. Effectively the same as a 2-for-1 stock split.

d. The earnings not paid out in dividends.

e. The stock price divided by earnings per share.

f. Summarizes the changes in the balance in each stockholders' equity account over a period of time.

g. Priced low in relation to current earnings.

h. Measures the ability of company management to generate earnings from the resources that owners provide.

i. Shows the balance in each equity account at a point in time.

j. The corporation's own stock that it reacquired.

Name _____ Date _____ Course _____ Section _____

Problem 10-2B

Requirement 1

March 1, 2012   **Debit**   **Credit**

_____   _____   _____

            _____   _____   _____

            _____   _____   _____

            _____

April 1, 2012

_____   _____

            _____   _____   _____

            _____   _____   _____

            _____   _____

June 1, 2012

_____   _____

            _____   _____   _____

            _____   _____

June 30, 2012

_____   _____

            _____   _____   _____

            _____

August 1, 2012

_____   _____

            _____   _____   _____

            _____

The McGraw-Hill Companies   *Financial Accounting*

Name _____ Date _____ Course _____ Section _____

Problem 10-2B Continued

October 1, 2012   Debit   Credit

_____   _____   _____

                                 _____   _____
                                 _____   _____
_____

Requirement 2

Transaction	Total Assets	Total Liabilities	Total Stockholders' Equity
Issue common stock			
Issue preferred stock			
Declare cash dividends			
Pay cash dividends			
Repurchase treasury stock			
Reissue treasury stock			

Problem 10-3B

	Before	After 100% Stock Dividend	After 2-for-1 Stock Split
Common stock, $0.01 par value			
Additional paid-in capital			
Total paid-in capital			
Retained Earnings			
Total stockholders' equity			
Shares outstanding			
Par value per share			
Share price			

Name _____ Date _____ Course _____ Section _____

Problem 10-4B

Requirement 1

_____

_____

Requirement 2

_____

_____

Requirement 3

_____

_____

_____

_____

Requirement 4

Retained Earnings, Beginning	
Retained Earnings, Ending	

_____

_____

Requirement 5

_____

_____

Requirement 6

_____

_____

 Financial Accounting

Problem 10-5B

Requirement 1

Nautical Balance Sheet (Stockholders' Equity Section) December 31, 2012	
Stockholders' equity:	
Total paid-in capital	
Total stockholders' equity	

Requirement 2

Nautical Statement of Stockholders' Equity For the Year Ended December 31, 2012						
	Preferred Stock	Common Stock	Additional Paid-in Capital	Retained Earnings	Treasury Stock	Total Stockholders' Equity
Balance, January 1						
Issued common stock						
Issued preferred stock						
Cash dividends						
Purchase treasury stock						
Reissue treasury stock						
Net income						
Balance, December 31						

Name _____ Date _____ Course _____ Section _____

Problem 10-5B Continued

Requirement 3

_____
_____
_____
_____
_____
_____
_____
_____
_____

Problem 10-6B

Requirement 1

<u>February 2, 2012</u>   Debit   Credit

_____   _____   _____

         _____   _____   _____

         _____   _____   _____

            _____   _____

<u>February 4, 2012</u>

_____   _____

         _____   _____   _____

         _____   _____   _____

            _____   _____

<u>June 15, 2012</u>

_____   _____

         _____   _____   _____

            _____   _____

Name _____ Date _____ Course _____ Section _____

Problem 10-6B Continued

<u>August 15, 2012</u>   Debit   Credit

_____   _____

                    _____   _____

                    _____   _____

                    _____

<u>November 1, 2012</u>

_____   _____

                    _____   _____

                    _____

<u>November 30, 2012</u>

_____   _____

                    _____   _____

                    _____

Requirement 2

National League Gear Balance Sheet (Stockholders' Equity Section) December 31, 2012	
Stockholders' equity:	
Total paid-in capital	
Total stockholders' equity	

 Financial Accounting

Name _____ Date _____ Course _____ Section _____

Problem 10-7B

Requirement 1

		÷		=	**Return on Equity**
Gap		÷		=	

_____
_____
_____

Requirement 2

		÷		=	**Return on the Market Value of Equity**
Gap		÷		=	

_____
_____
_____

Requirement 3

_____
_____
_____
_____
_____
_____
_____
_____
_____

Requirement 4

		÷		=	**Price-Earnings Ratio**
Gap		÷		=	

_____
_____
_____

The McGraw-Hill Companies *Financial Accounting*

Name _____ Date _____ Course _____ Section _____

Exercise 11-1

Items

_____ 1. Operating activities
_____ 2. Investing activities
_____ 3. Financing activities
_____ 4. Noncash activities
_____ 5. Indirect method
_____ 6. Direct method
_____ 7. Depreciation expense
_____ 8. Cash return on assets

Descriptions

a. Begins with net income and then lists adjustments to net income in order to arrive at operating cash flows.
b. Item included in net income, but excluded from net operating cash flows.
c. Net cash flows from operating activities divided by average total assets.
d. Cash transactions involving lenders and investors.
e. Cash transactions involving net income.
f. Cash transactions for the purchase and sale of long-term assets.
g. Purchase of long-term assets by issuing stock.
h. Shows the cash inflows and outflows from operations such as cash received from customers and cash paid for inventory, salaries, rent, interest and taxes.

Exercise 11-2

Name _____ Date _____ Course _____ Section _____

Exercise 11-3

	Section of the statement of cash flows
1. Purchase of a patent.	_____
2. Depreciation expense.	_____
3. Decrease in accounts receivable.	_____
4. Issuance of a note payable.	_____
5. Increase in inventory.	_____
6. Collection of notes receivable.	_____
7. Purchase of equipment.	_____
8. Exchange of long-term assets.	_____
9. Decrease in accounts payable.	_____
10. Payment of dividends.	_____

Exercise 11-4

	Section of the statement of cash flows
1. Issues $20 million in bonds.	_____
2. Purchases equipment for $80,000.	_____
3. Pays a $20,000 account payable.	_____
4. Collects a $15,000 account receivable.	_____
5. Exchanges land for a new patent. Both are valued at $300,000.	_____
6. Declares and pays a cash dividend of $100,000.	_____
7. Loans $50,000 to a customer, issuing a note receivable.	_____
8. Pays $75,000 to suppliers for inventory.	_____

Name _____ Date _____ Course _____ Section _____

Exercise 11-5

Perspective of Ernie's Electronics :

	Section of the statement of cash flows
1. Ernie sold Bert land, originally purchased for $180,000, at a sales price of $195,000, resulting in a gain on sale of land of $15,000.	_____
2. Ernie borrowed $100,000 from Bert signing a 3-year note payable.	_____
3. Ernie purchased $1 million in common stock in Bert's Bargain House through a private placement.	_____
4. Ernie received a dividend of $40,000 from the common stock investment in Bert's Bargain House.	_____

Exercise 11-6

Perspective of Bert's Bargain House :

	Section of the statement of cash flows
1. Ernie sold Bert land, originally purchased for $180,000, at a sales price of $195,000, resulting in a gain on sale of land of $15,000.	_____
2. Ernie borrowed $100,000 from Bert signing a 3-year note payable.	_____
3. Ernie purchased $1 million in common stock in Bert's Bargain House through a private placement.	_____
4. Ernie received a dividend of $40,000 from the common stock investment in Bert's Bargain House.	_____

Name _____ Date _____ Course _____ Section _____

Exercise 11-7

Technology Solutions Statement of Cash Flows For the Year Ended December 31, 2012		

Note: Noncash Activities		

Exercise 11-8

Cash Flows from Operating Activities		
Net cash flows from operating activities		

Name _____ **Date** _____ **Course** _____ **Section** _____

Exercise 11-9

Cash Flows from Operating Activities		
Net cash flows from operating activities		

_____

_____

_____

_____

_____

Exercise 11-10

Plasma Screens Corporation Statement of Cash Flows For the Year Ended December 31, 2012		
Cash Flows from Operating Activities		
Net cash flows from operating activities		
Cash Flows from Investing Activities		
Net cash flows from investing activities		
Cash Flows from Financing Activities		
Net cash flows from financing activities		
Net increase (decrease) in cash		
Cash at the beginning of the period		
Cash at the end of the period		

Name _____ Date _____ Course _____ Section _____

Exercise 11-11

Peach Computer Statement of Cash Flows For the Year Ended December 31, 2012		
Cash Flows from Operating Activities		
Net cash flows from operating activities		

Exercise 11-12

Requirement 1

	÷		=	**Return on Assets**
Google	÷		=	

_____

_____

Requirement 2

	÷		=	**Cash Return on Assets**
Google	÷		=	

_____

_____

Requirement 3

	÷		=	**Cash Flow to Sales**
Google	÷		=	
	÷		=	**Asset Turnover**
Google	÷		=	

The McGraw-Hill Companies

Name _____ Date _____ Course _____ Section _____

Exercise 11-12 Continued

_____
_____
_____
_____

Exercise 11-13

Peach Computer Statement of Cash Flows For the Year Ended December 31, 2012		
Cash Flows from Operating Activities		
Net cash flows from operating activities		

<u>**Calculations :**</u>

_____
_____
_____
_____
_____
_____
_____
_____
_____
_____
_____
_____
_____
_____
_____
_____
_____
_____
_____

Name _____ Date _____ Course _____ Section _____

Exercise 11-14

Cash received from customers :

Cash received from customers	

Cash paid to suppliers :

Cash paid to suppliers	

Cash paid for income taxes :

Cash paid for income taxes	

Exercise 11-15

Cash received from customers :

Cash received from customers	

Cash paid to suppliers :

Cash paid to suppliers	

Name _____ Date _____ Course _____ Section _____

Problem 11-1A

Type of Activity	Cash Inflow or Outflow	Transaction
_____	_____	1. Payment of employee salaries
_____	_____	2. Sale of land for cash
_____	_____	3. Purchase of rent in advance
_____	_____	4. Collection of an account receivable
_____	_____	5. Issuance of common stock
_____	_____	6. Purchase of inventory
_____	_____	7. Collection of notes receivable
_____	_____	8. Payment of income taxes
_____	_____	9. Sale of equipment for a note receivable
_____	_____	10. Issuance of bonds
_____	_____	11. Loan to another firm
_____	_____	12. Payment of a long-term note payable
_____	_____	13. Purchase of treasury stock
_____	_____	14. Payment of an account payable
_____	_____	15. Sale of equipment for cash

Name _____ Date _____ Course _____ Section _____

Problem 11-2A

ATM Software Developers Statement of Cash Flows For the Year Ended December 31, 2012		
Cash Flows from Operating Activities		
Net cash flows from operating activities		
Cash Flows from Investing Activities		
Net cash flows from investing activities		
Cash Flows from Financing Activities		
Net cash flows from financing activities		
Net increase (decrease) in cash		
Cash at the beginning of the period		
Cash at the end of the period		

Problem 11-3A

Alliance Technologies Statement of Cash Flows For the Year Ended December 31, 2012		
Cash Flows from Operating Activities		
Net cash flows from operating activities		

Name _____ Date _____ Course _____ Section _____

Problem 11-4A

Video Phones, Inc. Statement of Cash Flows For the Year Ended December 31, 2012		
Cash Flows from Operating Activities		
Net cash flows from operating activities		
Cash Flows from Investing Activities		
Net cash flows from investing activities		
Cash Flows from Financing Activities		
Net cash flows from financing activities		
Net increase (decrease) in cash		
Cash at the beginning of the period		
Cash at the end of the period		
Note: Noncash Activities		

Name _____ Date _____ Course _____ Section _____

Problem 11-5A

Requirement 1

	÷		=	Return on Assets
Google	÷		=	
Yahoo	÷		=	

_____
_____
_____

Requirement 2

	÷		=	Cash Return on Assets
Google	÷		=	
Yahoo	÷		=	

_____
_____
_____

Requirement 3

	÷		=	Cash Flow to Sales
Google	÷		=	
Yahoo	÷		=	

	÷		=	Asset Turnover
Google	÷		=	
Yahoo	÷		=	

_____
_____
_____
_____
_____
_____

Name _____ Date _____ Course _____ Section _____

Problem 11-6A

Alliance Technologies Statement of Cash Flows For the Year Ended December 31, 2012		
Cash Flows from Operating Activities		
Net cash flows from operating activities		

Calculations:

_____
_____
_____
_____
_____
_____
_____
_____
_____
_____
_____
_____
_____
_____
_____
_____
_____
_____
_____
_____
_____
_____
_____
_____
_____
_____
_____
_____
_____
_____
_____
_____
_____

Name _____ Date _____ Course _____ Section _____

Problem 11-7A

Video Phones, Inc. Statement of Cash Flows For the Year Ended December 31, 2012		
Cash Flows from Operating Activities		
Net cash flows from operating activities		
Cash Flows from Investing Activities		
Net cash flows from investing activities		
Cash Flows from Financing Activities		
Net cash flows from financing activities		
Net increase (decrease) in cash		
Cash at the beginning of the period		
Cash at the end of the period		
Note: Noncash Activities		

<u>Calculations :</u>

_____
_____
_____
_____
_____
_____
_____
_____
_____
_____
_____
_____
_____
_____

Problem 11-8A

Reverse Logic Income Statement For the Year Ended December 31, 2012		
Revenues		
Total Revenues		
Expenses:		
Cost of goods sold		
Operating expenses		
Depreciation expense		
Income tax expense		
Total expenses		
Net Income		

Revenues	
Change in accounts receivable	
Cash received from customers	

Cost of goods sold	
Change in inventory	
Purchases	
Change in accounts payable	
Cash paid to suppliers	

Operating expenses	
Change in prepaid rent	
Cash paid for operating expenses	

Income tax expense	
Decrease in income tax payable	
Cash paid for income taxes	

Problem 11-1B

Type of Activity	Cash Inflow or Outflow	Transaction
_____	_____	1. Issue common stock
_____	_____	2. Sale of land for cash
_____	_____	3. Purchase of treasury stock
_____	_____	4. Collection of an account receivable
_____	_____	5. Issuance of a note payable
_____	_____	6. Purchase of inventory
_____	_____	7. Repayment of a note payable
_____	_____	8. Payment of employee salaries
_____	_____	9. Sale of equipment for a note receivable
_____	_____	10. Issuance of bonds
_____	_____	11. Investment in bonds
_____	_____	12. Payment of interest on bonds payable
_____	_____	13. Payment of a cash dividend
_____	_____	14. Purchase of a building
_____	_____	15. Collection of a note receivable

Name _____ Date _____ Course _____ Section _____

Problem 11-2B

CPU Hardware Designers Statement of Cash Flows For the Year Ended December 31, 2012		
Cash Flows from Operating Activities		
Net cash flows from operating activities		
Cash Flows from Investing Activities		
Net cash flows from investing activities		
Cash Flows from Financing Activities		
Net cash flows from financing activities		
Net increase (decrease) in cash		
Cash at the beginning of the period		
Cash at the end of the period		

Problem 11-3B

Software Associates Statement of Cash Flows For the Year Ended December 31, 2012		
Cash Flows from Operating Activities		
Net cash flows from operating activities		

Name _____ Date _____ Course _____ Section _____

Problem 11-4B

Virtual Gaming Systems Statement of Cash Flows For the Year Ended December 31, 2012		
Cash Flows from Operating Activities		
Net cash flows from operating activities		
Cash Flows from Investing Activities		
Net cash flows from investing activities		
Cash Flows from Financing Activities		
Net cash flows from financing activities		
Net increase (decrease) in cash		
Cash at the beginning of the period		
Cash at the end of the period		

Note: Noncash Activities		

Name _____ Date _____ Course _____ Section _____

Problem 11-5B

Requirement 1

	÷		=	**Return on Assets**
Hewlett-Packard	÷		=	
IBM	÷		=	

_____
_____
_____

Requirement 2

	÷		=	**Cash Return on Assets**
Hewlett-Packard	÷		=	
IBM	÷		=	

_____
_____
_____

Requirement 3

	÷		=	**Cash Flow to Sales**
Hewlett-Packard	÷		=	
IBM	÷		=	

	÷		=	**Asset Turnover**
Hewlett-Packard	÷		=	
IBM	÷		=	

_____
_____
_____
_____
_____
_____
_____

Name _____ Date _____ Course _____ Section _____

Problem 11-6B

Software Associates Statement of Cash Flows For the Year Ended December 31, 2012		
Cash Flows from Operating Activities		
Net cash flows from operating activities		

Calculations:

_____
_____
_____
_____
_____
_____
_____
_____
_____
_____
_____
_____
_____
_____
_____
_____
_____
_____
_____
_____
_____
_____
_____
_____
_____
_____
_____
_____
_____
_____
_____

Name _____ Date _____ Course _____ Section _____

Problem 11-7B

Virtual Gaming Systems Statement of Cash Flows For the Year Ended December 31, 2012		
Cash Flows from Operating Activities		
Net cash flows from operating activities		
Cash Flows from Investing Activities		
Net cash flows from investing activities		
Cash Flows from Financing Activities		
Net cash flows from financing activities		
Net increase (decrease) in cash		
Cash at the beginning of the period		
Cash at the end of the period		

Note: Noncash Activities		

<u>Calculations :</u>

_____
_____
_____
_____
_____
_____
_____
_____
_____
_____
_____
_____
_____
_____

The McGraw-Hill Companies *Financial Accounting*

Name _____ Date _____ Course _____ Section _____

Problem 11-8B

Electronic Transformations Income Statement For the Year Ended December 31, 2012		
Revenues		
Expenses:		
Total expenses		
Net Income		

Revenues	
Change in accounts receivable	
Cash received from customers	

Operating expenses	
Change in accounts payable	
Cash paid for operating expenses	

Income tax expense	
Change in income tax payable	
Cash paid for income taxes	

The McGraw-Hill Companies   *Financial Accounting*

Exercise 12-1

Items

_____ 1. Vertical analysis
_____ 2. Horizontal analysis
_____ 3. Liquidity
_____ 4. Solvency
_____ 5. Discontinued operation
_____ 6. Extraordinary item
_____ 7. Quality of earnings
_____ 8. Conservative accounting practices

Descriptions

a. A company's ability to pay its current liabilities.
b. Accounting choices that result in reporting lower income, lower assets, and higher liabilities.
c. A profit or loss unusual in nature and infrequent in occurrence.
d. The ability of reported earnings to reflect the company's true earnings as well as the usefulness of reported earnings to help investors predict future earnings.
e. A tool to analyze trends in financial statement data for a single company over time.
f. The sale or disposal of a significant component of a company's operations.
g. A means to express each item in a financial statement as a percentage of a base amount.
h. A company's ability to pay its long-term liabilities.

Exercise 12-2

FEDERER SPORTS APPAREL				
Income Statement				
For the Years Ended December 31				
	2013		2012	
	Amount	%	Amount	%
Revenues				
Gross profit				
Net income				

Name _____ Date _____ Course _____ Section _____

Exercise 12-3

FEDERER SPORTS APPAREL Income Statement For the Years Ended December 31				
	Year		Increase (Decrease)	
	2013	2012	Amount	%
Revenues				
Gross profit				
Net income				

Exercise 12-4

Requirement 1

FEDERER SPORTS APPAREL Balance Sheet December 31				
	2013		2012	
	Amount	%	Amount	%
Total assets				
Total liabilities and stockholders' equity				

Name _____ Date _____ Course _____ Section _____

Exercise 12-4 Continued

Requirement 2

FEDERER SPORTS APPAREL Balance Sheet December 31				
	Year		Increase (Decrease)	
	2013	2012	Amount	%
Total assets				
Total liabilities and stockholders' equity				

Exercise 12-5

Requirement 1

<u>Risk Ratios</u>

Receivable turnover ratio = ——————————————— = —————

Average collection period = ——————————————— = —————

Inventory turnover ratio = ——————————————— = —————

Average days in inventory = ——————————————— = —————

Current ratio = ——————————————— = —————

Debt to equity ratio = ——————————————— = —————

Name _____ Date _____ Course _____ Section _____

Exercise 12-5 Continued

Requirement 2

_____
_____
_____
_____
_____
_____

Exercise 12-6

Requirement 1

Profitablity Ratios

Gross profit ratio   = _____   = _____

Return on assets   = _____   = _____

Profit margin   = _____   = _____

Asset turnover   = _____   = _____

Return on equity   = _____   = _____

Requirement 2

_____
_____
_____
_____
_____
_____
_____
_____

Name _____ Date _____ Course _____ Section _____

Exercise 12-7

Requirement 1

<u>Risk Ratios</u>

a. Receivable turnover ratio = ——————————————— = —————————

b. Inventory turnover ratio = ——————————————— = —————————

c. Current ratio = ——————————————— = —————————

d. Acid-test ratio = ——————————————— = —————————

e. Debt to equity ratio = ——————————————— = —————————

Requirement 2

_____
_____
_____
_____
_____
_____
_____
_____
_____
_____
_____
_____
_____
_____
_____
_____

The McGraw-Hill Companies *Financial Accounting*

Name _____ Date _____ Course _____ Section _____

Exercise 12-8

Requirement 1

Profitability Ratios

a. Gross profit ratio   = _____   = _____

b. Return on assets   = _____   = _____

c. Profit margin   = _____   = _____

d. Asset turnover   = _____   = _____

e. Return on equity   = _____   = _____

Requirement 2

_____
_____
_____
_____
_____
_____
_____
_____
_____
_____
_____
_____
_____
_____

Name _____ **Date** _____ **Course** _____ **Section** _____

Exercise 12-9

Requirement 1

<u>Profitability Ratios</u>

a. Gross profit ratio = ——————————————— = —————

b. Return on assets = ——————————————— = —————

c. Profit margin = ——————————————— = —————

d. Asset turnover = ——————————————— = —————

e. Return on equity = ——————————————— = —————

Requirement 2

————————————————————————————————————
————————————————————————————————————
————————————————————————————————————
————————————————————————————————————
————————————————————————————————————
————————————————————————————————————
————————————————————————————————————

Exercise 12-10

<u>Profitability Ratios</u>

Return on assets = ——————————————— = —————

Profit margin = ——————————————— = —————

Asset turnover = ——————————————— = —————

Return on equity = ——————————————— = —————

Name _____ Date _____ Course _____ Section _____

Exercise 12-11

	Classification	Brief Justification
a.	_____	_____
b.	_____	_____
c.	_____	_____
d.	_____	_____
e.	_____	_____
		_____
		_____

Exercise 12-12

LEBRON'S BOOKSTORES Income Statement For the Year Ended December 31, 2012	
Revenues	
Gross profit	
Net income	

Exercise 12-13

SHAQUILLE CORPORATION Income Statement For the Year Ended December 31, 2012	
Income before tax	
Income from continuing operations	
Net income	

Name _____ Date _____ Course _____ Section _____

Exercise 12-14

_____

Conservative / Aggressive

a. Increase the allowance for uncollectible accounts.

_____

b. When costs are going up, change from LIFO to FIFO.

_____

c. Change from the straight-line method of depreciation to declining balance in the second year of equipment with a ten year life.

_____

d. Record a smaller expense for warranties.

_____

Exercise 12-15

Requirement 1

a. _____

b. _____

c. _____

d. _____

e. _____

_____

_____

_____

Requirement 2

_____

_____

_____

_____

_____

_____

_____

_____

Name _____ Date _____ Course _____ Section _____

Problem 12-1A

Requirement 1

<table>
<tr><td colspan="5" align="center">SPORTS EMPORIUM
Income Statement
For the Years Ended December 31, 2012</td></tr>
<tr><td></td><td colspan="2" align="center">Sporting Goods</td><td colspan="2" align="center">Sports Apparel</td></tr>
<tr><td></td><td align="center">Amount</td><td align="center">%</td><td align="center">Amount</td><td align="center">%</td></tr>
<tr><td>Sales</td><td></td><td></td><td></td><td></td></tr>
<tr><td></td><td></td><td></td><td></td><td></td></tr>
<tr><td>Gross profit</td><td></td><td></td><td></td><td></td></tr>
<tr><td></td><td></td><td></td><td></td><td></td></tr>
<tr><td></td><td></td><td></td><td></td><td></td></tr>
<tr><td></td><td></td><td></td><td></td><td></td></tr>
<tr><td></td><td></td><td></td><td></td><td></td></tr>
<tr><td></td><td></td><td></td><td></td><td></td></tr>
<tr><td>Net income</td><td></td><td></td><td></td><td></td></tr>
</table>

Requirement 2

_____
_____
_____
_____
_____
_____
_____
_____
_____
_____
_____
_____
_____
_____
_____
_____
_____
_____
_____

Name _____ Date _____ Course _____ Section _____

Problem 12-2A

Requirement 1

| SPORTS EMPORIUM Income Statement For the Years Ended December 31 | | | |
| | | Increase (Decrease) | |
	2013	2012	Amount	%
Sales				
Gross profit				
Net income				

Requirement 2

_____
_____
_____
_____
_____
_____
_____
_____
_____
_____
_____
_____
_____

Name _____ Date _____ Course _____ Section _____

Problem 12-3A

Requirement 1

VIRTUAL GAMING SYSTEMS Balance Sheet December 31, 2012				
	2012		2011	
Assets	Amount	%	Amount	%
Current assets:				
Total assets				
Liabilities and Stockholders' Equity				
Current liabilities:				
Stockholders' equity:				
Total liabilities and equity				

Name _____ Date _____ Course _____ Section _____

Problem 12-3A Continued

Requirement 2

VIRTUAL GAMING SYSTEMS Balance Sheet December 31, 2012				
	Year		Increase (Decrease)	
Assets	**2012**	**2011**	**Amount**	**%**
Current assets:				
Long-term assets:				
Total assets				
Liabilities and Stockholders' Equity				
Current liabilities:				
Stockholders' equity:				
Total liabilities and equity				

The McGraw-Hill Companies *Financial Accounting*

Name _____ **Date** _____ **Course** _____ **Section** _____

Problem 12-4A

Risk Ratios

1. Receivable turnover ratio   =   _____   =   _____

2. Average collection period   =   _____   =   _____

3. Inventory turnover ratio   =   _____   =   _____

4. Average days in inventory   =   _____   =   _____

5. Current ratio   =   _____   =   _____

6. Acid-test ratio   =   _____   =   _____

7. Debt to equity ratio   =   _____   =   _____

8. Times interest earned ratio   =   _____   =   _____

Problem 12-5A

Profitability Ratios

1. Gross profit ratio   =   _____   =   _____

2. Return on assets   =   _____   =   _____

3. Profit margin   =   _____   =   _____

4. Asset turnover   =   _____   =   _____

5. Return on equity   =   _____   =   _____

6. Price-earnings ratio   =   _____   =   _____

Name _____ Date _____ Course _____ Section _____

Problem 12-6A

Requirement 1

Risk Ratios

Receivable turnover ratio

2012 = _____ = _____

2013 = _____ = _____

Inventory turnover ratio

2012 = _____ = _____

2013 = _____ = _____

Current ratio

2012 = _____ = _____

2013 = _____ = _____

Debt to equity ratio

2012 = _____ = _____

2013 = _____ = _____

Name _____ Date _____ Course _____ Section _____

Problem 12-6A Continued

Requirement 2

<u>Profitability Ratios</u>

Gross profit ratio

    2012   = _____ = _____

    2013   = _____ = _____

Return on assets

    2012   = _____ = _____

    2013   = _____ = _____

Profit margin

    2012   = _____ = _____

    2013   = _____ = _____

Asset turnover

    2012   = _____ = _____

    2013   = _____ = _____

Requirement 3

_____

_____

_____

_____

_____

_____

Name _____ Date _____ Course _____ Section _____

Problem 12-1B

Requirement 1

	GAME-ON SPORTS Income Statements For the Year Ended December 31, 2012			
	Athletic Equipment		Accessories	
	Amount	%	Amount	%
Sales				
Gross profit				
Net income				

Requirement 2

_____

_____

_____

_____

_____

_____

_____

Problem 12-2B

Requirement 1

	GAME-ON SPORTS Income Statements For the Year Ended December 31			
			Increase (Decrease)	
	2013	2012	Amount	%
Sales				
Gross profit				
Net income				

The McGraw-Hill Companies *Financial Accounting*

Name _____ Date _____ Course _____ Section _____

Problem 12-2B Continued

Requirement 2

_____
_____
_____
_____
_____
_____

Problem 12-3B

Requirement 1

THE ATHLETIC ATTIC Balance Sheet December 31				
	2012		**2011**	
Assets	**Amount**	**%**	**Amount**	**%**
Current assets:				
Long-term assets:				
Total assets				
Liabilities and Stockholders' Equity				
Current liabilities:				
Stockholders' equity:				
Total liabilities and equity				

 Financial Accounting

Problem 12-3B Continued

Requirement 2

THE ATHLETIC ATTIC Balance Sheet December 31				
	Year		Increase (Decrease)	
Assets	2012	2011	Amount	%
Current assets:				
Long-term assets:				
Total assets				
Liabilities and Stockholders' Equity				
Current liabilities:				
Stockholders' equity:				
Total liabilities and equity				

 Financial Accounting

Name _____ Date _____ Course _____ Section _____

Problem 12-4B

Risk Ratios

1. Receivable turnover ratio   = ————————————— = ————————

2. Average collection period   = ————————————— = ————————

3. Inventory turnover ratio   = ————————————— = ————————

4. Average days in inventory   = ————————————— = ————————

5. Current ratio   = ————————————— = ————————

6. Acid-test ratio   = ————————————— = ————————

7. Debt to equity ratio   = ————————————— = ————————

8. Times interest earned ratio   = ————————————— = ————————

Problem 12-5B

Profitability Ratios

1. Gross profit ratio   = ————————————— = ————————

2. Return on assets   = ————————————— = ————————

3. Profit margin   = ————————————— = ————————

4. Asset turnover   = ————————————— = ————————

5. Return on equity   = ————————————— = ————————

6. Price-earnings ratio   = ————————————— = ————————

Name _____ Date _____ Course _____ Section _____

Problem 12-6B

Requirement 1

<u>Risk Ratios</u>

Receivable turnover ratio

2012   = _____ = _____

2013   = _____ = _____

Inventory turnover ratio

2012   = _____ = _____

2013   = _____ = _____

Current ratio

2012   = _____ = _____

2013   = _____ = _____

Debt to equity ratio

2012   = _____ = _____

2013   = _____ = _____

Name _____ Date _____ Course _____ Section _____

Problem 12-6B Continued

Requirement 2

<u>**Profitability Ratios**</u>

Gross profit ratio

2012 = _____ = _____

2013 = _____ = _____

Return on assets

2012 = _____ = _____

2013 = _____ = _____

Profit margin

2012 = _____ = _____

2013 = _____ = _____

Asset turnover

2012 = _____ = _____

2013 = _____ = _____

Requirement 3

_____
_____
_____
_____
_____
_____
_____
_____
_____
_____

Name _____ Date _____ Course _____ Section _____

Exercise C-1

	Investment amount	Interest rate	Compounding	Period invested	Future value
Jerry	_____	_____	_____	_____	_____
Elaine	_____	_____	_____	_____	_____
George	_____	_____	_____	_____	_____
Kramer	_____	_____	_____	_____	_____

_____
_____

Exercise C-2

Initial investment	Annual rate	Interest compounded	Period invested	Future value
_____	_____	_____	_____	_____

Exercise C-3

	Contract amount	Discount rate	Compounding	Period invested	Present value
Derek	_____	_____	_____	_____	_____
Isabel	_____	_____	_____	_____	_____
Meredith	_____	_____	_____	_____	_____
George	_____	_____	_____	_____	_____

Exercise C-4

	Purchase amount	Discount rate	Compounding	Period due	Present value
Store 1	_____	_____	_____	_____	_____
Store 2	_____	_____	_____	_____	_____

Name _____ Date _____ Course _____ Section _____

Exercise C-5

	Payment in one year	Discount rate	Compounding	Present value	Payment today	Total cost
Option 1	_____	_____	_____	_____	_____	_____
Option 2	_____	_____	_____	_____	_____	_____
Option 3	_____	_____	_____	_____	_____	_____

_____
_____

Exercise C-6

	Annuity payment	Annual rate	Interest compounded	Period invested	Future value of annuity
Option 1	_____	_____	_____	_____	_____
Option 2	_____	_____	_____	_____	_____
Option 3	_____	_____	_____	_____	_____

Exercise C-7

Annuity payment	Annual rate	Interest compounded	Period invested	Future value of annuity
_____	_____	_____	_____	_____

Exercise C-8

	Annuity payment	Annual rate	Interest compounded	Period invested	Present value of annuity
Option 1	_____	_____	_____	_____	_____
Option 2	_____	_____	_____	_____	_____

_____
_____
_____

Name _____ Date _____ Course _____ Section _____

Problem C-1A

Person	Age	Initial investment	Accumulated investment by retirement (age 65)
Alec			
Daniel			
William			
Stephen			

Problem C-2A

	Annuity payment	Discount rate	Interest compounded	Period invested	Present value of annuity
Years 1-6					

	Future value	Discount rate	Interest compounded	Period invested	Present value
Year 7					
Year 8					
Year 9					
Year 10					
Year 10					

C-4

Name _____ **Date** _____ **Course** _____ **Section** _____

Problem C-3A

Camera 1:

	Annuity payment	Discount rate	Interest compounded	Period invested	Present Value of annuity
Years 1-8	_____	_____	_____	_____	_____

	Future value	Discount rate	Interest compounded	Period invested	Present value
Year 8	_____	_____	_____	_____	_____

Total cost of camera 1 = _____

Camera 2:

	Future value	Discount rate	Interest compounded	Period invested	Present value
Year 3	_____	_____	_____	_____	_____
Year 5	_____	_____	_____	_____	_____
Year 7	_____	_____	_____	_____	_____

Total cost of camera 2 = _____

_____
_____
_____
_____
_____

© 2011   The McGraw-Hill Companies   *Financial Accounting*

Name _____ Date _____ Course _____ Section _____

Problem C-1B

Requirement 1 and 2

Person	Annuity payment	Type of account	Expected annual return	Five-year accumulated investment	Maximum home purchase
Mary Kate					
Ashley					
Dakota					
Elle					

Problem C-2B

	Annuity payment	Discount rate	Interest compounded	Period invested	Present value of annuity
Years 1-15					

	Future value	Discount rate	Interest compounded	Period invested	Present value
Year 15					

Present value of future cash flows = _____

_____

_____

Name _____ Date _____ Course _____ Section _____

Problem C-3B

Option 1:

Present value   = _____

Option 2:

	Annuity payment	Discount rate	Interest compounded	Period invested	Present value of annuity
Years 1-10	_____	_____	_____	_____	_____

Present value   = _____

Option 3:

	Annuity payment	Discount rate	Interest compounded	Period invested	Present value of annuity
Years 1-10	_____	_____	_____	_____	_____

Present value   = _____

Option 4:

	Future payment	Discount rate	Interest compounded	Period invested	Present Value
Year 5	_____	_____	_____	_____	_____

Present value   = _____

_____

_____

_____

_____

_____

Name _____ **Date** _____ **Course** _____ **Section** _____

Exercise D-1

_____ 1. A reason companies invest in other companies is to build strategic alliances.

_____ 2. All companies are required to pay dividends to their investors.

_____ 3. When market interest rates increase, the market value of a bond increases as well.

_____ 4. One way for a company to expand operations into a new industry is to acquire the majority of another company's common stock that already operates in that industry.

_____ 5. Stocks typically have greater upside potential, providing a higher average return to their investors over the long-run than do bonds.

_____ 6. Companies purchase debt securities primarily for the dividend revenue they provide.

Exercise D-2

Requirement 1

December 20   **Debit**   **Credit**

_____   _____

                    _____   _____

                    _____

December 28

_____   _____

                    _____   _____

                    _____

December 31

_____   _____

                    _____   _____

                    _____

The McGraw-Hill Companies   *Financial Accounting*

Name _____ Date _____ Course _____ Section _____

Exercise D-2 Continued

Requirement 2

_____

_____
_____
_____

Exercise D-3

Requirement 1

February 1	Debit	Credit
_____	_____	_____
_____		_____
_____		_____

June 15		
_____	_____	
_____	_____	
_____		_____
_____		

October 31		
_____	_____	
_____		_____
_____		

December 31		
_____	_____	
_____		_____
_____		_____

Name _____ Date _____ Course _____ Section _____

Exercise D-3 Continued

Requirement 2

_____

_____

_____

_____

Investments

Exercise D-4

Requirement 1

March 1	Debit	Credit
_____	_____	
_____	_____	
_____		_____

July 1

_____	_____	
_____		_____
_____		_____

October 1

_____	_____	
_____		_____
_____		_____
_____		_____

December 31

_____	_____	
_____		_____

Name _____ Date _____ Course _____ Section _____

Exercise D-4 Continued

Requirement 2

_____
_____
_____
_____

Investments

Exercise D-5

Requirement 1

_____
_____
_____
_____
_____
_____
_____
_____
_____
_____
_____
_____
_____
_____

Requirement 2

Sales Revenue	
Comprehensive income	

Name _____ Date _____ Course _____ Section _____

Exercise D-6

<u>January 1, 2012</u>   **Debit**   **Credit**

_____   _____

     _____   _____

     _____   _____

<u>December 31, 2012</u>

_____   _____

     _____   _____

<u>December 31, 2012</u>

_____   _____

     _____   _____

     _____   _____

Exercise D-7

<u>January 1, 2012</u>   **Debit**   **Credit**

_____   _____

     _____   _____

     _____

<u>December 31, 2012</u>

_____   _____

     _____   _____

     _____   _____

Name _____ Date _____ Course _____ Section _____

Exercise D-7 Continued

December 31, 2012   Debit   Credit

_____   _____

            _____   _____

            _____

Exercise D-8

Requirement 1

Purchase: Debit   Credit

_____   _____

            _____   _____

            _____

Net income:

_____   _____

            _____   _____

Dividends:

_____   _____

            _____   _____

            _____

Fair value adjustment:

_____   _____

            _____   _____

            _____

Name _____ Date _____ Course _____ Section _____

Exercise D-8 Continued

Requirement 2

<u>Purchase:</u>   **Debit**   **Credit**

_____   _____   _____

_____   _____

_____   _____

<u>Net income:</u>

_____

_____   _____

_____   _____

<u>Dividends:</u>

_____

_____   _____

_____   _____

<u>Fair value adjustment:</u>

_____

_____   _____

_____   _____

Name _____ Date _____ Course _____ Section _____

Exercise D-9

_____ 1. 10% of the common stock of Beta.

_____ 2. 40% of the bonds of Gamma.

_____ 3. 75% of the common stock of Delta.

_____ 4. 15% of the bonds of Epsilon.

_____ 5. 25% of the common stock of Zeta.

_____ 6. 60% of the bonds of Eta.

_____ 7. 100% of the common stock of Theta.

Exercise D-10

Requirement 1

(1) Date	(2) Cash Received	(3) Interest Revenue	(4) Increase in Carrying Value	(5) Carrying Value

Requirement 2

<u>January 1, 2012</u>   Debit _____   Credit _____

_____   _____

_____   _____

_____

The McGraw-Hill Companies   *Financial Accounting*

Name _____ Date _____ Course _____ Section _____

Exercise D-10 Continued

June 30, 2012   ___Debit___   ___Credit___

_____   _____
_____   _____

                                                                         _____   _____

                                                                         _____

December 31, 2012

_____   _____
_____   _____

                                                                         _____   _____

                                                                         _____

Exercise D-11

Requirement 1

(1) Date	(2) Cash Received	(3) Interest Revenue	(4) Increase in Carrying Value	(5) Carrying Value

Requirement 2

January 1, 2012   ___Debit___   ___Credit___

_____   _____

                                           _____   _____

                                           _____

The McGraw-Hill Companies   *Financial Accounting*

Name _____ Date _____ Course _____ Section _____

Exercise D-11 Continued

June 30, 2012   Debit   Credit

_____   _____

                    _____   _____

                    _____   _____

                    _____

December 31, 2012

_____   _____

                    _____   _____

                    _____   _____

                    _____

Name _____ Date _____ Course _____ Section _____

Problem D-1A

Requirement 1

<u>January 2, 2012</u>   Debit   Credit

_____   _____

_____   _____

_____   _____

<u>February 14, 2012</u>

_____   _____

_____   _____

_____   _____

<u>May 15, 2012</u>

_____   _____

_____   _____

_____   _____

_____   _____

<u>December 30, 2012</u>

_____   _____

_____   _____

_____

<u>December 31, 2012</u>

_____   _____

_____   _____

_____

Name _____ Date _____ Course _____ Section _____

Problem D-1A Continued

<u>December 31, 2012</u>   **Debit**   **Credit**

_____   _____   _____

_____   _____   _____

Requirement 2

_____

_____

_____

_____

_____

_____

Problem D-2A

<u>Purchase:</u>   **Debit**   **Credit**

_____   _____   _____

_____   _____   _____

_____   _____   _____

<u>Net income:</u>

_____   _____   _____

_____   _____   _____

<u>Dividends:</u>

_____   _____   _____

_____   _____   _____

_____

Name _____ Date _____ Course _____ Section _____

Problem D-3A

Requirement 1

(1) Date	(2) Cash Received	(3) Interest Revenue	(4) Increase in Carrying Value	(5) Carrying Value

Requirement 2

__January 1, 2012__   Debit   Credit

_____   _____

_____   _____

_____   _____

__June 30, 2012__

_____   _____

_____   _____

_____   _____

_____   _____

__December 31, 2012__

_____   _____

_____   _____

_____   _____

_____   _____

Name _____ Date _____ Course _____ Section _____

Problem D-3A Continued

Requirement 3

<u>December 31, 2012</u>   Debit   Credit

_____   _____   _____

_____   _____   _____

_____   _____

Requirement 4

_____

_____

_____

_____

_____

Problem D-4A

Requirement 1

                                                         Debit   Credit

_____   _____

          _____   _____

          _____

Requirement 2

                                                         Debit   Credit

_____   _____

_____   _____

          _____   _____

          _____

Name _____ Date _____ Course _____ Section _____

Problem D-4A Continued

Requirement 3

	Debit	Credit
_____	_____	
_____	_____	
_____		_____
_____		

Requirement 4

_____
_____
_____
_____
_____
_____
_____
_____
_____
_____
_____
_____
_____
_____
_____
_____
_____
_____
_____

Name _____ Date _____ Course _____ Section _____

Problem D-1B

Requirement 1

<u>February 2, 2012</u>   **Debit**   **Credit**

_____

_____

_____

<u>February 4, 2012</u>

_____

_____

_____

<u>July 15, 2012</u>

_____

_____

_____

_____

<u>December 30, 2012</u>

_____

_____

_____

<u>December 31, 2012</u>

_____

_____

_____

Name _____ Date _____ Course _____ Section _____

Problem D-1B Continued

<u>December 31, 2012</u>   **Debit**   **Credit**

_____ _____ _____

_____ _____ _____

Requirement 2

_____

_____

_____

_____

Problem D-2B

<u>Purchase:</u>   **Debit**   **Credit**

_____ _____

_____ _____

_____ _____

<u>Net income:</u>

_____ _____

_____ _____ _____

_____

<u>Dividends:</u>

_____ _____

_____ _____ _____

_____

Name _____ Date _____ Course _____ Section _____

Problem D-3B

Requirement 1

(1) Date	(2) Cash Received	(3) Interest Revenue	(4) Increase in Carrying Value	(5) Carrying Value

Requirement 2

<u>January 1, 2012</u>   Debit   Credit

_____   _____

_____   _____   _____

_____

<u>June 30, 2012</u>

_____   _____

_____   _____

_____   _____

_____

<u>December 31, 2012</u>

_____   _____

_____   _____

_____   _____

_____

               Financial Accounting

Name _____ Date _____ Course _____ Section _____

Problem D-3B Continued

Requirement 3

<u>December 31, 2012</u>   Debit   Credit

_____   _____
_____   _____

          _____   _____
          _____

Requirement 4

_____
_____
_____
_____
_____
_____

Problem D-4B

Requirement 1

                                                              Debit   Credit

_____   _____

          _____   _____
          _____

Requirement 2

                                                              Debit   Credit

_____   _____
_____   _____

          _____   _____
          _____

Name _____ Date _____ Course _____ Section _____

Problem D-4B Continued

Requirement 3

	Debit	Credit
_____	_____	_____
_____	_____	_____
_____		_____
_____		

Requirement 4

_____

_____

_____

_____

_____

_____

_____

_____

_____

_____

_____

_____

_____

_____

_____

_____

The McGraw-Hill Companies *Financial Accounting*

Name _____ Date _____ Course _____ Section _____

Exercise E-1

	Reason		**Description**

1. _____ Legal system

2. _____ Tax laws

3. _____ Sources of financing

4. _____ Inflation

5. _____ Culture

6. _____ Political and economic ties

7. _____ Economic development

a. More-developed economies have more complex business transactions.

b. The extent of public disclosure depends on the secretiveness of society.

c. Common law countries rely more heavily on public information.

d. Countries share business activities and have political connections.

e. Alignment between financial reporting and tax reporting rules.

f. In some countries, asset values increase rapidly because of the general price level changes.

g. Some countries rely more heavily on debt capital than on equity capital to fund operations.

Exercise E-2

Requirement 1

Austria

Reason	**Options**

1. _____ Legal system — (a) Common-law / (b) Code-law

2. _____ Tax laws — (a) Different tax and financial accounting rules / (b) Similar tax and financial accounting rules

3. _____ Sources of financing — (a) More equity financing / (b) More debt financing

4. _____ Inflation — (a) Low inflation / (b) High inflation

5. _____ Culture — (a) Transparent / (b) Secretive

6. _____ Political and economic ties — (a) British ties / (b) German ties / (c) Spanish ties

The McGraw-Hill Companies *Financial Accounting*

Name _____ Date _____ Course _____ Section _____

Exercise E-2 Continued

	Reason	Options
7. _____	Economic development	(a) Developed economy (b) Developing economy (c) Under-developed economy

Requirement 2

Australia

	Reason	Options
1. _____	Legal system	(a) Common-law (b) Code-law
2. _____	Tax laws	(a) Different tax and financial accounting rules (b) Similar tax and financial accounting rules
3. _____	Sources of financing	(a) More equity financing (b) More debt financing
4. _____	Inflation	(a) Low inflation (b) High inflation
5. _____	Culture	(a) Transparent (b) Secretive
6. _____	Political and economic ties	(a) British ties (b) German ties (c) Spanish ties
7. _____	Economic development	(a) Developed economy (b) Developing economy (c) Under-developed economy

Name _____ Date _____ Course _____ Section _____

Exercise E-3

For :

_____
_____
_____
_____
_____
_____
_____
_____
_____
_____

Against :

_____
_____
_____
_____
_____
_____
_____
_____
_____
_____
_____
_____

Exercise E-4

Requirement 1

_____
_____
_____
_____

Requirement 2

_____
_____

Requirement 3

_____
_____
_____
_____

The McGraw-Hill Companies *Financial Accounting*

Name _____ Date _____ Course _____ Section _____

Exercise E-4 Continued

Requirement 4

_____
_____
_____
_____
_____
_____

Exercise E-5

Requirement 1

_____
_____
_____
_____
_____
_____
_____

Requirement 2

(a) _____
_____

(b) _____
_____

(c) _____
_____
_____

Requirement 3

(a) _____
_____

(b) _____
_____
_____

(c) _____
_____
_____

Name _____ Date _____ Course _____ Section _____

Exercise E-6

Requirement 1

Date	Transaction	Number of units	Unit Cost	Ending Inventory
Jan. 1	_____	_____	_____	_____
Apr. 7	_____	_____	_____	_____

Date	Transaction	Number of units	Unit Cost	Cost of Goods Sold
Apr. 7	_____	_____	_____	_____
Oct. 9	_____	_____	_____	_____

Gross profit = _____ − _____

= _____ − _____

=

Requirement 2

Date	Transaction	Number of units	Unit Cost	Ending Inventory
Oct. 9	_____	_____	_____	_____

Date	Transaction	Number of units	Unit Cost	Cost of Goods Sold
Jan. 1	_____	_____	_____	_____
Apr. 7	_____	_____	_____	_____
Oct. 9	_____	_____	_____	_____

Gross profit = _____ − _____

= _____ − _____

=

Name _____ Date _____ Course _____ Section _____

Exercise E-6 Continued

Requirement 3

_____
_____
_____
_____
_____

Exercise E-7

Requirement 1

_____
_____
_____
_____
_____

Requirement 2

_____
_____
_____
_____
_____
_____
_____
_____

Requirement 3

_____
_____
_____
_____
_____

Name _____ Date _____ Course _____ Section _____

Exercise E-8

Requirement 1

_____
_____
_____
_____

Requirement 2

_____
_____
_____
_____
_____
_____
_____
_____
_____
_____
_____

Requirement 3

_____
_____
_____
_____
_____
_____
_____
_____

Requirement 4

_____
_____
_____
_____
_____
_____
_____
_____
_____
_____
_____